I0796825

THE 5 HABITS OF HOPE

THE 5 HABITS OF HOPE

STORIES & STRATEGIES TO HELP YOU FIND YOUR WAY

DR. JULIA GARCIA

This book is not intended to provide therapy, counseling, or clinical advice or treatment, or to take the place of clinical advice and treatment from your own personal physician. Readers are advised to consult their own qualified health-care physicians regarding medical issues. Neither the publisher nor the author takes any responsibility for the possible consequence from any treatment, action, or application of information in this book to the reader.

Some names and identifying characteristics have been changed to protect the privacy of individuals.

The 5 Habits of Hope

Copyright © 2025 Dr. Julia Garcia

All rights reserved. No portion of this book may be reproduced, stored in a retrieval system, or transmitted in any form or by any means—electronic, mechanical, photocopy, recording, scanning, or other—except for brief quotations in critical reviews or articles, without the prior written permission of the publisher.

Published by Harper Celebrate, an imprint of HarperCollins Focus LLC.

Any internet addresses (websites, blogs, etc.) in this book are offered as a resource. They are not intended in any way to be or imply an endorsement by HarperCollins Focus LLC, nor does HarperCollins Focus LLC vouch for the content of these sites for the life of this book.

Interior design: Sabryna Lugge and Emily Ghattas
Author photo: John Castillo
Cover design: Micah Kandros

ISBN 978-1-4002-5085-1 (HC)
ISBN 978-1-4002-5088-2 (audiobook)
ISBN 978-1-4002-5086-8 (epub)

Printed in India

25 26 27 28 29 MAN 5 4 3 2 1

CONTENTS

A Note of Hope vii
Introduction: We Need More Hope viii

PART ONE: FROM HOPELESS TO HOPEFUL 1

1 My Story 2
2 Our Stories 12
3 The Social Shift 28
4 Health and Hope 44
5 Introducing the Five Habits of Hope 58

PART TWO: THE FIVE HABITS OF HOPE 75

6 Habit #1: Reflect 76
7 Habit #2: Risk 94
8 Habit #3: Release 120
9 Habit #4: Receive 144
10 Habit #5: Repurpose 166

Dear Reader 186
Notes 188
About the Author 196

A Note of Hope

Who are we to speak of hope?

For those who have nearly drowned in the depths of despair,
having to run as fast and far away as possible
to keep from staying there.

If hopelessness has ever been a hole
you called home,
know
wherever you are
with hope,
you will never be alone.

For you,
who may feel hopeless now,
you are still here,
and so is hope.

It is yours if you'll have it.
I hope you will.

Sincerely,
Dr. Julia

INTRODUCTION

WE NEED MORE HOPE

It's powerful, optimistic, lifesaving, melodramatic, ultra-ambiguous, and elusive. It's for everyone, yet, holding on to it can feel impossible.

Hope, by definition, is the expectation of a belief fulfilled, but there isn't a universal understanding of it. Some argue it's a feeling; others say it's a theory or a choice. Scientists share that it's a cognitive process and a science.

In the upcoming chapters, we'll explore the nuances of hope—the science behind it, society's struggle with it, and why it's needed now more than ever—but for now, let's consider how we *feel* about it.

If I were to ask what hope means to you, chances are you wouldn't give me a dictionary definition. Because hope, in the end, comes down to a feeling. You know it when you have it. You feel it when you don't.

Similar to a revolving door, hope enters one moment, then escapes right back out the next. When hope is gone, it can negatively impact our physical and mental health.[1] The opposite is also true. Hope is the single best predictor of well-being compared to any other measure of trauma recovery.[2]

Throughout the book, we will discover that having more hope can positively impact our lives. It won't solve every issue we face, such as deep trauma or chronic illness, but it can help us on our journey of healing.

If hope is so powerful, why is it so difficult to hold on to?

HOPE BLOCKS

For nearly two decades, my work as a social scientist has given me a unique perspective on the significance of hope. I have witnessed its ability to heal, and I have seen up close the harm that can happen when it is absent.

As I searched for more clarity about the connection between hope and health, I noticed that we don't go from hopeful to hopeless overnight. We don't just wake up one day and suddenly feel like quitting our jobs, giving up, or running away from a situation. Something often gets in the way. Sometimes it's clear; other times it's so subtle you might not even notice it. I refer to these obstacles as "hope blocks."

Hope blocks are the different barriers that keep us from feeling hopeful. The barriers can be personal or shared, obvious or outside of our peripheral view. They can increase in size depending on hardships, such as trauma, loss, financial strains, mental illnesses, diagnoses, and other situations that affect our well-being. Each barrier gets stuck in our way, driving a wedge between where we are and where we aspire to be. They further perpetuate the touch-and-go feeling of hope.

A few of the hope blocks we see in society include a growing surge in anxiety and feelings of loneliness affecting our youth,[3] with suicide being the second-leading cause of death for youth and young adults.[4] In addition to that, nearly 5 percent of the global population is suffering from depression.[5] More tools to process our emotions are needed, arguably now more than ever.

Without a process for navigating difficult hardships and developing healthy emotional habits, feeling hopeful can be difficult. The circumstances we face make this challenging, along with the emotional habits we've developed around them, such as negative self-talk or suppressing our feelings. Strengthening our arsenal of emotional tools moves us toward hope. The best tools we have at our disposal are also the biggest hope blocks—*our feelings*.

FLIPPING THE SCRIPT ON FEELINGS

I'm a psychologist, but probably not the kind you're picturing. My "office" is often thirty thousand feet in the air as I travel to my speaking events, where my clients aren't individuals sitting on a couch—they're groups of people, as few as thirty or numbering in the thousands.

I've devoted my career to helping people heal and rediscover hope through these diverse spaces and tools, and it doesn't always look the same. Sometimes it means developing technology to help workplace teams navigate conflict and foster connection. Other times, it's working with organizations to create programming that transforms how they approach mental health and fosters a more engaged and passionate culture.

This varied work has brought me to millions of people worldwide, and one thing has become clear: We're not all taught how to deal with our feelings or build systems to help us move through them. The problem with not having tools is that healing—and hope—feel out of reach or can quickly escape our grasp when we need them most. My mission is to change that.

When we develop a process, the psychological strength of hope can lessen feelings of despair and be a protective resource for coping with stress and adversity.[6] The opposite is also true. Our health and relationships suffer without a process to navigate our emotional terrain. Implementing a process gives us an internal tool kit.

The challenge is that we often approach feelings like anxiety or stress by focusing on external factors—things that are beyond our control. But when we flip the script, shifting our attention from external circumstances to our internal world, we can build hope-based habits to navigate our feelings. The obstacles that block hope can then be turned into stepping stones, from barriers into building blocks, from setbacks into steps forward.

If hope blocks are never addressed, and feelings are never processed, the barriers pile up. For some, a profound apathy replaces any belief that life can improve. Hopelessness becomes a hole they call home. Nestled inside, it feels impossible to leave.

I know all too well what that hole, that feeling of hopelessness, can be like.

Throughout this book, we will be exploring delicate topics, stories of hope, and feelings of hopelessness through the lens of personal experience and behavioral science. While the tools, frameworks, and processes shared have been essential in my own journey of healing and hope—and I hope they will serve you in yours as well—they are not a replacement for traditional therapeutic services.

I recognize, however, that therapeutic and medical services aren't always preferred, accessible, or affordable. These pages are meant to encourage you wherever you are.

This book isn't here to tell you what to hope for either. It's meant to support you in discovering that for yourself. Think of the concepts shared throughout each chapter as dots on a blank canvas. You decide where to fill in the spaces and how to connect the dots. Add your own texture and colors along the way. Building habits of hope is about designing your own masterpiece.

PART ONE

FROM HOPELESS TO HOPEFUL

ONE

MY STORY

I was initially reluctant to take hope seriously because of the depths of despair I had been to. What's more, I had seen others through their darkest hours, and too many of them never made it through. Even as I write this, I am navigating a loved one's mental illness becoming debilitating, a friend's painful divorce, and the death of a close friend from suicide.

Hopelessness, I get.

I've felt its sinking claws mining my confidence, convincing me I am not good enough. I've sought refuge from its polarizing lens on my relationships, telling me I don't deserve real love. I've climbed out of its wreckage after my self-worth was stripped bare from shame.

Though I had plenty of reasons to lose hope in hope, I see that it is everywhere, and its essence is undeniable. From small things, like the friend who says, "I hope you feel better," to bigger emotional pulls, like the internal voice hoping your children are safe when you drop them off at school—hope is all around us, whether we believe in its transformative power or not.

When I look over at my husband, son, and newborn baby, I can't help but feel the very hope I used to struggle to see the validity in. These moments of having hope help get me through.

THE POWER OF MOMENTS

Twenty-four to thirty-six hours is the typical amount of time I spend traveling to and from speaking events away from my family. Ninety minutes is what I usually get when I'm facilitating a workshop, and it's normally one hour for a keynote. Forty-five minutes if I'm meeting one-on-one with a client, and thirty if I'm having an introductory call with a leader from a prospective client organization. Twenty minutes is the usual time spent in conversation with someone who has reached out through a crisis hotline. Fifteen minutes to share what I do at conferences through a showcase-style format such as TEDx. Two minutes is the average time dedicated to taking audiences through The Five Habits of Hope writing framework.

All these moments, collectively, work for one purpose—to build hope. These moments are what I work for. In a single moment of realization, the entire trajectory of our lives can shift. In one moment, we can accept an offer to college, hear a newborn's first cry, lock eyes with our soulmates, or press Send on our two-weeks' notices to our employers. A moment—whether of realization, decision-making, or something deeper—can alter the course of our lives.

NO PLACE FOR IMPERFECT PARTS

I first understood the power of a moment when my life was at risk—a moment where one decision could have changed everything. When that moment arose, it felt like a force within me and also completely beyond my control—like the wind, embodying both chaos and calm.

I learned early in my life that the world preferred calm, cool, and collected over seeing the imperfect parts of a person. As a result, for most of my life, I was paralyzed by fear, doubt, and the constant need to control the storm inside me. I'd hide its current under complacent restraint. I'd waive my desire to be seen if it meant my storm would have to be known too.

I was conflicted, torn between being my authentic self with all my imperfections and portraying a perpetual image of resilience and perfection. I noticed that the more I personified perfection, the more I was entrusted with increasing responsibilities and seen as a leader. At first, this social validation felt gratifying. However, it came at a cost. There was little room for failure. Worse, there was no space for both chaos and calm to be seen—no space to be the real, not-so-pretty me—imperfect parts and all.

Being rewarded for presenting a false pretense only reinforced my belief that insecurities and fears were unacceptable. *I never thought I was enough.* This had a hugely detrimental effect on me. In fact, it led me to believe that the world would be better off without me.

ON THE EDGE OF DESPAIR

I never imagined being alive long enough to see my twenties. I didn't dream of growing old or having a family with a home and a white picket fence surrounding it. High school was the first time I struggled with suicide ideation, and in one moment, I went as far as attempting to take my own life. I didn't want to burden anyone—I just wanted to disappear. I wasn't sure I deserved a future.

This fear of never being enough followed me everywhere. It felt like I was dangling off a cliff, gripping a slippery indent in a rock above with one hand while my other was restrained by a rope tied behind my back. I was hanging on but held back. My feelings told me I should give up.

I was on the edge of despair. No one knew the internal suffering I was going through. I had learned to bury these feelings so deep that no evidence could surface.

By the time I entered college, I was running full speed, chasing highs to avoid feeling the lows. I would seek any high-risk adrenaline rush and the thrill of being on the edge of danger.

One Saturday night, I took things too far. My cousin Shaun had recently died at nineteen from a methadone overdose, and the emotions I had been suppressing around it—rage, sadness, confusion—came to a crashing head. I ended up taking a significant mix of oxycodone, hard liquor, and marijuana in a short period.

Before I knew it, I had blacked out. This wasn't anything new for me. I had ventured into those dark hallways before. This time was different though. When I came to, friends told me I had gotten into a fight and been in a cop car chase, and word had reached my college athletic director. I was suspended from my sports team, where I was on scholarship, sent to mandatory counseling for the year, and strongly advised to attend outpatient rehab, which I reluctantly did.

At this point, I still hated being open about my feelings, especially in a room where other people could witness. I was more afraid of showing feelings than of putting myself in danger. I thought if I did share emotions, I'd be weak. Nothing could've been worse.

As much as I wanted to, it felt impossible to heal from everything broken inside me. Fear of opening up was holding a death grip on my heart. I needed to believe everything could be better. I needed to *feel* hopeful again.

NO HEALING WITHOUT HOPE

By the end of the rehab program and school semester, I managed to stop drinking and doing drugs, but I didn't feel much different about who I was. I had learned to cut out some not-so-healthy and dangerous behavioral habits, but I still refused to open up emotionally. The way I felt about myself hadn't improved. I still felt worthless. But at this point, I was stripped of my usual tactics to avoid these feelings. If pain, shame, or even despair resurfaced, I still didn't know what to do with these feelings. Whenever I tried to pry shame away from my sense of worth, the shattered fragments seemed to tear deeper into my flesh.

How could I help myself if I hated myself? As far as I could tell, behavior modification wasn't changing that. External factors weren't going to change me from the inside. Not yet, anyway. Not without a process to hope and a way to navigate the feelings that were blocking me from it.

Beforehand, hope felt as elusive as the wind. I may have occasionally felt its rush wrapping around my shoulders, but just as quickly, it would dissipate. I needed to create space to find and hold on to hope. Rather than try and control or catch the wind, I needed to develop a process to harness it.

This is when the internal rebuilding began.

REBUILDING HOPE BY CREATING NEW HABITS

After that blackout, things had to change if I was going to make it off the edge of despair. I couldn't go on repeating the same emotional habits that were hurting me any longer. Since I had spent the first part of my life without any practice for handling my emotions—facing feelings wasn't a subject taught in school or discussed at the dinner table—I had my work cut out for me.

To climb out of the wreckage of worthlessness, I set out to rebuild my life with different emotional and behavioral habits. It started with being ready to confront the conflicting and complicated ebb and flow—the constant cycle of feeling hopeful one moment and then feeling numb from the emptiness it leaves behind the next.

My strategy: seek knowledge. *How were others handling it all?* I read everything from the Bible to any self-help book I could get my hands on. I studied and researched relentlessly, eventually earning a PhD in psychology. There was a wealth of information, and much of it was very helpful in understanding my mind and rewiring my thought patterns.

However, I recognized that academic knowledge could take me only so far. If I wasn't careful, I could easily use knowledge as another method to mask my emotions, pretending I had it all figured out when, in reality, I didn't. I needed real, full-heart experiences. I needed spaces where I could drop the mask, be fully honest with myself, and engage with my feelings. I needed to get in the habit of reflecting.

I had to find the courage to face what I hid behind, but I knew I couldn't do it alone—or maybe I just didn't want to anymore. I decided to take a risk in relationships, too, and another habit began to build: the habit of risking. It was crucial to surround myself with a few close friends I could open up to, seek professional counseling, and attend public support groups. I also took a risk in my faith and began attending church regularly, praying, and pouring my shame and soul into the pews.

Writing became a lifeline as well. Some days, I wrote as if my life depended on it—and on many days, it felt like it did. Through this expression, I discovered the power of cultivating the habit of releasing. This written release allowed my suppressed thoughts a place to untangle and breathe. Eventually, the words evolved into another form of release through spoken word poetry.

By opening up and creating more space in my heart, I made room for the habit of receiving. I allowed myself to be open to what would help me—mindset tools, professional counsel, more meaningful relationships, an upgraded sense of worth, and different physical outlets for my stress and anger. My lifestyle was permitting healthy outlets for once. I replaced taking shots at the bar until I blacked out on Friday nights with drinking ginger shots on Saturday mornings to improve my gut health. Rather than running away from my problems, I ran along New York's Hudson River on weeknights. I stopped using myself as a punching bag and started training in a boxing gym, sparring with professionals instead.

Hope and healing became more than just my journey; they went on to inspire my professional pursuits. I discovered creative ways to channel feelings of pain and injustice. These emotions became fuel, igniting innovation and sparking new ideas for solving problems—the habit of repurposing was in motion.

I took the pain I felt from my cousin Shaun's drug overdose and channeled it into prevention work, traveling the country and bringing drug awareness programming to college and university campuses. Repurposing feelings of pain to fuel my pursuits didn't stop there either. I went on to create award-winning technology for addressing mental health on social media and a digital tool to combat bias and inequity surrounding civil unrest. I built training programs for leadership and mental health, conducted research on health and culture, and launched a suicide crisis hotline, all while touring hundreds of cities as a keynote speaker.

I didn't realize it then, but through these five new habits—reflecting, risking, releasing, receiving, and repurposing—I established more ways to manage emotions, deepen relationships, and pursue professional passions, all while cultivating hope.

HABITS OF HOPE

Through unrelenting trials and errors, I learned how rebuilding my life required a framework for processing my internal world. Allowing space for the built-up emotions I had carried for years to surface and be channeled outward became a practice. This shift created a clear path for hope to build a new home in my heart. Before, the suppression of my emotions was crushing me; now, the processing of my emotions was creating new habits—*habits of hope*.

The key to this process was that the new habits were both external *and* internal. Once I established internal habits, the external ones stuck. Beforehand, whenever I had made a behavior change, it felt temporary and separate from who I was because there was no emotional buy-in for me to keep it going.

Now, what I did and who I wanted to be were finally aligning. These new habits of navigating my emotions were equipping me to face hardship and myself head-on without losing hope. I said goodbye to the girl who chased danger and masked her pain. In her place, I welcomed an empowered version of myself—someone worthy of both hope and healing. I found a way to develop a habit of processing my feelings and, ultimately, to face myself—and the feelings that blocked hope in the first place.

My own journey of healing and hope has not been an easy or straight-arrow path. There have been many curves and setbacks. Several I share in this book. The key for me was creating a *process* to navigate my feelings. In doing so, I was able to build and implement habits of hope.

Despite all the barriers to hope, building emotional practices helped me heal. These habits transformed my health and well-being. My life grew in the most unforeseen ways. I went from being someone who refused to open up and didn't believe she deserved to be alive to someone with a strong sense of worth, sharing vulnerably on stages around the world.

Since then, I have had the privilege of traveling the world—skydiving over open deserts, riding waves in Hawaii, soaking in the sunsets of Dubai, dancing in Acapulco, biking the cobbled streets of Europe, zip-lining cliff tops in Tulum, riding a train through the Swiss Alps, indulging in Peruvian cuisine, and drinking water from glaciers in Iceland. All while working with people of all ages and from every kind of background, helping them navigate their journeys toward healing and hope.

Despite it all, and against all odds, hope saved me. It set me free.

Not only did I make it out of my twenties alive, but I also have faith and hope in Jesus Christ, which is the foundation for everything I do. I now have a beautiful, growing family who has supported me every step of the way. We even have a home with a white picket fence.

Habits of hope changed the course of my life, and for years, I have seen how they've helped others. Now, as you explore your own story, I am hopeful they can help you too!

TWO

OUR STORIES

I had just wrapped up a sixty-minute keynote speech to empower student leaders at Johns Hopkins University, and the floor opened for questions. Nearly a thousand people were in the audience, but I quickly saw an eager hand in the front row go up.

Once given a microphone, this student described an overwhelming cultural climate in which they felt defeated: "With all the wars going on, the politics, academic pressures, social media pressures, anxiety, and climate change, it feels like we're all doomed." After a brief pause and exasperated sigh, they continued, "How do we stay *hopeful* through it all?"

Here was a student enrolled in one of the most prestigious universities in the world, known for its rigorous academic programs, and they wanted to talk about hope. And I get it. If we consider all that is happening around us, this world can feel doomed, or at least deeply broken.

According to the National Alliance on Mental Illness (NAMI), over 50 percent of employees are feeling burned out,[1] a state of emotional exhaustion that continues to escalate. As this burnout rises, so does the rate at which technology and automation are replacing countless jobs. Beyond the career field, issues extend into communities and homes, where housing properties are becoming unaffordable for the masses. In 2022, 70 percent of Americans reported they couldn't afford the same kind of homes and education their parents did.[2]

To add even more doom and gloom, drug-related overdoses are the deadliest they've ever been.[3] This is not to mention the global conflicts and wars, climate change, increased rates of depression, the rampant rise of anxiety,[4] and suicide rates that are at a thirty-year high.[5]

Yes, it's hard to see the hope in it all.

But over the past two decades, I have seen and experienced up close hope elevating individuals and communities in the midst of the most difficult circumstances and trying times. My work has brought me to the very center of those asking the question: To hope or not to hope?

The unique front-row seat I've had working across hundreds of cities has given me a clear view of the battle between hope and its adversary, hopelessness. I've experienced the tension of standing at the crossroads and choosing which direction to take. I've seen it personally, culturally, and globally.

It has never mattered what the topic of a speaking event is or the audience I am working with, one question is always surfacing: Where do we find hope?

HUNGRY? HAPPY? HOPEFUL?

Toward the beginning of my career as a speaker, I was invited to work with an alternative high school in Phoenix, Arizona. Before I arrived, I'd been cautioned that the students I would be working with had been labeled "at-risk" because many of them had been expelled from public school, were on probation, or had extenuating life circumstances that made traditional learning environments ineffective.[6] I was warned they would be "tough" kids who would probably never open up to me or anyone else.

Knowing this, I decided to forgo a traditional speech and wanted to just get real, real quick. Before even introducing myself, I began the workshop by writing a wide range of words on the whiteboard: *tired*, *hungry*, *happy*, *hopeful*, *bored*, *afraid*, and more. And then I simply asked the students to jot down which words they could relate to at that moment.

After a few minutes, I encouraged anyone who wanted to share to explain what they wrote. To my surprise and to the surprise of the school director, almost all the hands went up. This writing exercise opened the emotional gates of a group of teens who were deemed "unreachable." With guided facilitation, these students shared everything—from being afraid of not graduating from high school to being angry about a father who had left years before.

I was floored by the depth of participation. And afterward, these students shared that the writing prompt and exercise allowed them to become more hopeful. Some even went on to identify various goals they wanted to achieve, such as graduating from high school or being the first in their family to go to college. Through this exercise, I saw that these students were not only hurting but also hungry for hope. The experience opened my eyes in a new way.

I began to forgo a traditional storytelling approach in my speaking events and instead dedicated a significant amount of time to facilitating the processing of the audience's stories through various exercises, including writing prompts. In doing so, participants were sharing, in their own words, things I would have never known by reading statistics. They described everything from overwhelming pressures to grief, abuse, struggles with doubt, fear, anxiety, and suicidal ideation.

Since then, I've facilitated thousands of exercises in which participants actively build tools to process their emotions in real time, opening up in ways I had never seen before. Their bold vulnerability has shattered any preconception I had that when feelings are expressed, it's a sign of weakness. Their shared stories give me strength. I hope they'll also encourage you.

WHY SHARED STORIES MATTER

Throughout these pages, you will see anonymous stories from individuals who've gone through my exercise on this journey toward hope. Many of these stories have been heartbreaking, but they all show a deep-seated conviction that, in a single moment, we can experience something that gives us hope to keep going.

The stories represent diverse voices and lived experiences, unfiltered and in their own words. They offer a glimpse of unvarnished vulnerability, like a brief page of a diary tucked under a bed frame. They show us what it looks like to open up and share the things we may not be able to say out loud.

They also let us know we are not alone.

For instance, in this collection of stories below—ranging from a youth in Arizona to a young adult in Los Angeles to a soon-to-be-retired educator in New Orleans—do you see a common theme?

I struggled because I felt alone.
I felt hopeless.

I struggled because my dad became a alcoholic and drug addict and went to jail.
I felt hopeless. Unworthy.

I struggled because of my depression.
I felt hopeless and worthless.

I struggle with having hope and motivation to live.
I feel alone and useless.
I need someone to care.

I STRUGGLED BECAUSE I LOST MY MOM AND ALMOST LOST MY SON.
I FELT *HOPELESS* AND EMPTY.

When I read these handwritten responses after an event I'm facilitating, I'm overwhelmingly aware of two things: feelings of loneliness and hopelessness. And this is just a small sample of many more responses like them.

It's very clear to me that our culture is in a crisis of disconnection and despair. Because of this, we are not only in need of hope but also the emotional practices to sustain it.

A CULTURE IN CRISIS

Year after year, I've become inundated with raw, heartrending responses like those I just shared. The more I've gathered, the clearer the dots between despair and disconnection have become. Regardless of whether individuals share experiences of abuse, loss, or a lack of confidence, they communicate similar feelings. Across every demographic I've worked with, the overwhelming theme of the handwritten stories has been the absence of hope.

Feeling lost, stuck, or alone are symptoms of a growing problem taking root in our inner worlds. The more I looked, the more evidence I discovered surrounding the internal crisis of disconnection and despair and how the two are connected.

DISCONNECTION ⇄ DESPAIR

In order to make sense of this, let's define *despair* and *crisis*.

Despair is another word for "hopelessness," an emotional feeling in which improvement seems utterly impossible. Psychiatrist Viktor Frankl said it best when he defined despair as "suffering without meaning."[7] This helps us understand that sometimes there is no fault, rhyme, or reason to despair.

When we consider a "crisis," we may immediately think of a buzzing headline, but what does it mean when applied to ourselves and our inner worlds? At its core, a crisis is a system out of balance.

When I built a crisis training program during the height of the COVID lockdowns, I found an image of a seesaw to be the most helpful in explaining an internal crisis to our volunteer responders.

Let's consider how we spend our time, for example. Picture the seesaw distributing uneven weight on either side. On one end, it shows how a person spends time alone. On the other, it shows time spent in connection with others in person. When this balance is off—when we're alone more than with others—hope dips. Social connection is essential for emotional well-being. When it's lacking, we can experience an increase in levels of anxiety, depression, and hopelessness. When thinking about balance, consider these imbalances:

- *An imbalance of attention:* You're drained from spending more attention behind a screen than being present in person with loved ones and peers.
- *An imbalance of connection:* You're engaging on social media but not in a meaningful way, and you are left feeling more alone than ever.
- *An imbalance of hope:* You're looking at your life and the world and don't believe things will get better.

When hope is lacking, our emotional systems, particularly our mental health, can spiral into a crisis. And because an internal crisis can happen unexpectedly and often go unseen, we might not know someone is struggling until it's very far along or even becomes dangerous. We may be surprised to find out our closest married friends are living separately or our child's teammate attempted suicide. Unfortunately, just like disconnection can lead to despair, the opposite can be true too—despair can lead to disconnection. When we are in a crisis, we may not seek the connection we need and attempt to carry the burden alone. (In chapter 9, we'll identify helpful indicators of when someone may be struggling and ways to support them.)

In surveying thousands of students from high schools to universities across hundreds of cities, I learned three primary reasons why people won't open up about their struggles:

1. They don't want to look weak.
2. They don't want to be a burden.
3. They don't want to worry anyone.

I stayed silent because I didn't want to be a burden.

When we suppress emotions long enough, we run out of room to hold them, leading to an internal crisis. We get overwhelmed with feelings that have yet to be worked through, and they end up taking over, regardless of whether we like it or are even aware it is happening. At some point, discouragement takes over, and we don't believe things can improve.

Recognizing this imbalance is a powerful step toward healing. Being aware of an unhealthy behavior pattern, however, does not give us an answer about how to solve it. But acknowledging the imbalance is a great place to start. As we take steps toward breaking unhealthy emotional patterns (habits), we will see this process is not about perfection but progression.

LET GO AND LET IN

One of my favorite sounds is the rustling of paper. At the end of my speaking events, I invite participants to pass their handwritten stories forward if they want to let go of what they have written—their struggles, their fears, their unmet dreams, and the burdens they had been carrying for years. As the pages are folded and sorted, I witness how the act of letting go makes space for hope to restore balance.

The collective act of hundreds or even thousands of students, teachers, staff, business leaders, and parents alike sharing their stories—physically handing them over—is a remarkable experience. The sound of papers shuffling together as they are being passed forward shifts the energy in the room. Hope is palpable. And it has a sound.

After these events, participants have expressed feeling less alone and more hopeful that their lives could improve. Many described it as "freeing" to see their peers opening up alongside them. It became clear to me how important it is to make space for processing life's hardest moments. I saw something unexpected and amazing happen in unlikely places—classrooms, boardrooms, prisons, and beyond. Hope was emerging.

My experience contrasted sharply with what I was seeing in the culture. Here, there was freedom to be authentic, vulnerable, and open. There was no fakeness or filter. Countless individuals were breaking free from cycles of suppression, genuinely opening up and forming meaningful connections. The collective voice of so many people was saying, "I don't want to go through this alone anymore."

And with that collective voice ringing in my ears, after a decade of having a front-row seat to emotional breakthroughs, an alarm set off inside me. I knew I needed to share this with the world.

HOPE EMERGED

This book is the culmination of years of research, observation, and living testimonies—my own and others'—that it's possible to move from hopeless to hopeful. My own process of building habits of hope started as a way to survive and navigate my emotions. After years of my own healing journey and a decade in academia, the habits I developed evolved into exercises I designed for the audiences I speak to.

They became The Five Habits of Hope.

These habits are largely in response to the countless personal stories that have been shared with me over the years, and they provide practical tools for you to use in your own life.

Of course, not everyone's path is the same. The route to hope and healing isn't linear. Remember, you fill the space however you need. I have discovered that the more we hold space for stories to be shared authentically and without judgment, the more hope hangs in the air like oxygen. We don't always notice the role it plays in our lives, but it's always around us.

Honing these five habits gives us confidence that if we ever find ourselves dangling for dear life on the edge of despair—wanting to give up on our dreams, relationships, or even ourselves—we are prepared. We can engage these processes much like a parachute strapped to our back. We won't fall off the edge of despair. We will rise and soar in both expectation and belief.

Hope will emerge.

I am hopeful for my future.

I am hopeful for . . . continued growth in that area and peace and happiness.

I am hopeful for a change in myself.

I AM HOPEFUL FOR MY ABILITY TO CARE FOR MYSELF.

RESTORING BALANCE

After collecting hundreds of thousands of handwritten responses, I made a discovery: Hope is an antidote to our crisis of disconnection and despair. But in order for it to have a lasting and effective impact on individuals and in our culture, we need a process for sustaining it. We need a way to hold on to it through a series of emotional habits.

With the escalation of mental health issues in our society and the link between depression and suicide, building hope is critical and can even be lifesaving. Having hope makes way for more healing. When emotional processing becomes a regular practice—the way we prioritize nutrition or physical routines—we develop an innate tool kit.

Each time another person chooses to build a process toward hope, the internal crisis levels out. As they do, the weight of that balance shifts toward hopefulness, fueling their journey to keep moving forward. With more hope, we are likely to resolve conflicts in relationships, perform better at work, and pursue our passions, among many other benefits that we will continue to explore in the book.

As we unpack The Five Habits of Hope, know that they are less about having hope all the time and more about always having a clear process for navigating yourself back toward it.

PREPARING WITH A PROCESS

Remember the story of the student at Johns Hopkins University who asked how to hold on to hope amid hardship? They were expressing how vital hope was to their personal journey. They recognized how hope matters when facing anxiety, social pressures, or even civil unrest.

When I responded to their question, I shared where we can start building hope: "There is a space between hopelessness and hope. This space is where most of us find ourselves when faced with challenges." And this is the best space to prepare a process for hope.

Remember, hope and emotions are intrinsically intertwined. This is why we need tools to navigate our emotions before we can expect to hold on to hope. Most of us already follow emotional patterns; we just may not realize it yet. To modify their course, these preset emotional patterns need space to be reexamined and rerouted if needed.

Hope isn't just something you find; it's something you *build* over and over again, using methods you can learn and apply daily. Building hope is about having space to process and navigate our mental wellness—a series of mental health habits for both our minds and actions.

When I was struggling with grief, feelings of unworthiness, and even suicide ideation, I desperately needed hope but didn't know how to hold on to it. That's when habits of hope created a way through.

For each habit, we will build practices to process feelings—what I call The Feeling Framework—preparing us to combat anything life throws our way. These habits and frameworks aren't quick solutions or a one-size-fits-all remedy for all our problems, but they offer a way to help us navigate challenges in our emotional processes.

THE FIVE HABITS OF HOPE ARE LESS ABOUT HAVING HOPE ALL THE TIME AND MORE ABOUT ALWAYS HAVING A CLEAR PROCESS FOR NAVIGATING YOURSELF BACK TOWARD IT.

THREE

THE SOCIAL SHIFT

Why do so many of us find it challenging to navigate emotions and stay hopeful? How did we get here? In order to understand better, let's take a wider look at the internal crisis of disconnection and despair we introduced earlier.

As a society, we are currently undergoing what I call a social shift: We've changed not only where we spend our time but also how we show up in those spaces. We are always online, plugged in, digitally and virtually connected. But because we are spending more time online than in person, our digital habits are greatly and negatively impacting our relationships.

Take a look at these real stories of individuals and see if you can identify common emotional struggles.

I felt *lonely*.
I was needing a friend.

I am struggling with being open.
I felt *alone*.

I struggled because I lost my mother to cancer.
I felt lost, alone, not understood.

I struggled because of my relationship.
I felt alone.

I STRUGGLED BECAUSE I DIDN'T KNOW THAT
I COULD OR SHOULD CALL FOR HELP.
I FELT SO ALONE.

As you can see, loneliness is everywhere. It's a universal feeling and a global concern. Even though we can feel like we're the only ones experiencing it, the ironic thing about loneliness is that so many people feel it at the same time. I hope seeing these stories from others reminds you that you are never alone.

LOOKING AT LONELY

You may not be personally struggling with your relationships and connections with others, but there are likely loved ones within your circle who are. We can't be afraid to talk about loneliness. Lives depend on us doing so.

Loneliness is often described as the subjective feeling of being isolated or disconnected from others, and it is a fundamental indicator of social well-being—or lack thereof.[1] As with hope, you can usually tell if you're feeling it or not, but you may not have a dictionary definition to explain what you're experiencing. You just know that you are lonely.

Feelings of loneliness can present themselves in different ways—the sting of emptiness after a breakup or a growing pit in your stomach after months of searching for a job with no prospects on the horizon. And it doesn't take long for loneliness to become the full-time stomping ground for grips of despair to take up residence. Without much warning, we can be lonely one moment and then feel utterly hopeless the next.

And loneliness does not discriminate.

A GLOBAL TREND

The Western world has never been more technologically developed, but amid the infinite portal of access and information is a growing sense of loneliness. Studies show loneliness has doubled since the 1980s[2] and nearly one in four adults feels lonely.[3] News reports call loneliness an epidemic, highlighting the significance with headlines like "Americans Are Lonely, and It's Killing Them."[4]

Research from the American Psychiatric Association revealed that one in three Americans experienced loneliness at least once a week over the past year,[5] raising the alarm from politicians and health professionals alike, including a US surgeon general who went on to issue a formal advisory to address the "epidemic." In it, he cited health risks from loneliness, including how it can be life-threatening, increasing the chance of early mortality upwards to 30 percent.[6]

The American Academy of Pediatrics has also made headlines with its findings, declaring a national emergency in child and adolescent mental health. They note soaring rates of depression, anxiety, trauma, loneliness, and suicidality that will have lasting impacts on them, their families, and their communities.[7]

With this growing global trend and the alarms being raised at the top levels, it's time we look closer at the societal change causing this epidemic, what I call a social shift.

THE SHIFT FROM IN PERSON TO ONLINE

What's driving this shift?

It's largely due to the time we spend in online communities. It's no secret that the internet has become a dominant aspect of our daily lives. But did you know that people around the world, including in the US, are using screens for about seven hours a day?[8] That's more hours than I get of sleep on a daily basis! Another study indicates that Americans check their phones a total of eight billion times a day; this is approximately every five minutes.[9]

This rapidly evolving digital landscape is replacing traditional social gathering spots like local pubs with virtual hubs. Digital communities are more frequented than neighborhood bookstores and local gyms. Platforms like Facebook, YouTube, Instagram, online gaming apps, and TikTok are hot spots for cultivating social connections, replacing everything from in-person workplace meetups to community church events. In fact, nearly 65 percent of the global population is on social media[10]—that's the majority of the planet!

This new world affects families in new ways too. Children are frequenting online gaming more than local playgrounds, and parents are swapping ideas on social media reels instead of at the local PTA (Parent Teacher Association). Adolescents are spending less unstructured time with friends in person and are now behind a screen on social media for nearly five hours a day.[11] All this points toward the new social shift—from meeting peers in person to meeting them online.

We are now part of a societal evolution, a changing of the guard in connectivity, the end of a non-digital era. A new chapter in history is unfolding, and it's looking more and more imbalanced.

IMBALANCED DIGITAL HABITS

Being online isn't the real issue; the problems we're facing are largely due to the imbalance of time spent online. Remember the seesaw we referenced to explain a crisis? We can apply this same concept to our digital habits.

Think of how you divide your time. Is it primarily online? When we look at the quantity of time spent alone on social media versus being with others in person, we begin to see a clear pattern of behavior; it's dangerously imbalanced.

My research shows similar results. People are spending significant time alone. While working with Penn State University, one thousand of their incoming freshmen shared how they spent an average of three to four hours a day alone, behind a screen. Fourteen percent reported being isolated for seven to eight hours a day.

Afterward, these same students shared where they would go if they were to reach out for help with a struggle they were experiencing. Only 1 percent were willing to open up on social media. The majority, 81 percent, said they would turn to a friend for support. This shows that even when we spend significant time on social media, it is not the place we turn to for real support when we're struggling.

This is not just a behavior among college students. As shown by the American Time Use Survey by the Census Bureau, Americans spend an average of two hours and forty-five minutes per week with friends, which is less than half the time spent with friends a decade ago.[12]

What do these digital habits have to do with our health? Leading experts and health professionals are discovering links between our online habits and declining mental health. We've already established how loneliness is an epidemic in our hyperconnected world and not something to be taken lightly.

Research indicates that for people who spend five or more hours a day on-screen, there are considerably higher risks of suicide and unhappiness.[13] Studies also show that using social media for doomscrolling is linked to decreased well-being over time.[14] Youth are among those who are particularly affected, with their use of the internet being linked to increased rates of anxiety, depression, suicidal ideation, and other mental health problems.[15]

Ultimately, digital connections may supplement in-person relationships, but they cannot take their place. This is perhaps why we are connected digitally yet feeling alone. An app on our phones won't wrap its digital arms around us. It does not replace a hug, a high five, a tone of voice, or facial expressions, even if artificial intelligence is getting freakishly close to being able to do so.

DIFFERENT KINDS OF DOPAMINE

Why are we drawn to social media when it causes us so much harm?

I first took a personal interest in social media's impact on health after conducting interviews with young adults about their own experiences with it in academia. In these interviews, I heard one heart-wrenching story after another from young people who were being sexually harassed and told unspeakable things online, such as "just die already." I couldn't fathom anyone having the nerve to say something like that, but then I learned it was being done behind a screen. The social dynamic had shifted.

There is a reason why social media steals so much of our attention. Every time a new notification appears—signaling another like, comment, or new post—it activates the reward pathway in our brains and releases dopamine. This surge of dopamine lights up our brains' reward system like fireworks, engaging the same neurological pleasure circuitry involved in addiction to nicotine, alcohol, or cocaine. Internet addiction can lead to structural changes in the brain and can have a detrimental impact on our cognitive functioning, which affects our attention span, emotional regulation, and self-control.[16]

When we apply the concept of dopamine release to hope, however, it's different from the dopamine releases we experience when we're online seeking external validation. Hope-based dopamine is tied to personal growth. Another key differentiator is the long-term effects: Hope-based habits release positive, purposeful change over time, whereas the dopamine we experience from social media can encourage superficial connections that cause anxiety or stress over time.

NOT ALL TIME ONLINE IS BAD

For many of us, our digital interactions are complicated. There is a lot we love about it, and some aspects can even be life-changing! Depending on how we use it, being online can heighten feelings of connection and build a sense of community. Friends in different cities can share a hearty laugh any time of day via an animated GIF on social media, while strangers can build lifelong friendships by connecting over like-minded interests and ideas.

Social media unlocks access to resources and allows us to raise awareness for causes we support with just a few clicks. In a remote village in Madagascar, a young teenager utilized a local internet café started by my husband and discovered YouTube. Within weeks, they learned how to play an instrument by watching video tutorials. That's the creative magic that can be sparked online.

Online communities are particularly beneficial for professional connections. They broaden access to clients and can grow professional networks. Social media enables business professionals to cross time zones and geographical limitations, making engaging with audiences quicker and more cost-effective.

Love can be online too. Social dating apps allow complete strangers an introduction, sometimes leading to a relationship. Thanks to some of these apps, several of my friends and family members have found their spouses and grown a family together. I've even officiated a wedding because of a match made online.

HEALTHY OR HURTFUL?

Since our relationships with digital communities are complicated, knowing when they become unhealthy or hurtful can be difficult. One moment, they can make us laugh out loud, feeling good about ourselves, and the next, we can experience such intense self-hatred from comparing ourselves to others that it brings us to tears.

In order to assess your own relationship with digital communities, ask yourself some of the following reflection questions:

- Are the social media and gaming apps I use designed with my mental health and well-being in mind?

- Do they hurt or help my relationships with those who matter most to me?
- Am I feeling anxious or more fulfilled from my time spent in online communities?

One of the ways we can evaluate whether our relationship with online communities is teetering toward harmful is to look at it in the way we would a potentially abusive relationship. The following table shows parallels between the warning signs of abusive behavior[17] and areas of concern on social media.

HOW HARMFUL IS OUR SOCIAL MEDIA?

ABUSIVE BEHAVIOR FROM A PARTNER
Your partner shows extreme jealousy of your friends or time spent away from them.
Your partner prevents or discourages you from spending time with others.
Your partner insults or demeans you, especially in front of other people.

HARM FROM SOCIAL MEDIA

You become extremely jealous of others and have endless FOMO (fear of missing out), sometimes doomscrolling for hours.

You spend time away from friends, family, and peers because of the addictive and distracting nature of social media. Plus, design features stimulate our brain's reward pathway, resulting in the release of dopamine (a pleasure producer). It's highly addictive.

You feel publicly insulted or demeaned by online harassment, hateful speech, or divisive rhetoric.

POTENTIAL CORRELATIONS

Both scenarios can intensify anxiety, insecurity, and self-doubt. In relationships, jealous partners can make you feel extreme guilt or anxiousness if you are not with them. On social media, the endless streams of picture-perfect lives, or curated highlight reels, can escalate feelings of inadequacy and trap insecurities in a cycle of comparison and anxiety.

Both scenarios can lead to social isolation. In abusive relationships, partners may try to cut you off from people you love and your social lifelines so that they can make you dependent on them. Social media has its own way of drawing us into an isolated world. The addictive nature and gamification can deepen our dependency on it, often at the expense of real-life support networks, deepening feelings of loneliness.

Both scenarios can result in emotional harm. Absusive partners may demean partners in front of others, using insults and shaming to undermine their self-esteem. On social media, public shaming and harssment can severely wound mental health and self-worth. The digital nature means the attacks could stay online indefinitely, amplifying feelings of helplessness.

If we don't periodically check on our social media use and potential dependency, we may find ourselves in an imbalanced state—seeking to connect through the very source that is potentially contributing to our loneliness. Being mindful of our behaviors makes way for us to restore balance if we need to.

Navigating the challenges around loneliness in today's day and age requires us to implement more hope-based processes that can restore balance in our digital habits. And we should keep in mind that social media is a neutral medium—its impact depends on how we use it. While this shift in social spaces will continue to spark intrigue, concern, and debate, one fact is overwhelmingly clear: An imbalance of time spent online can lead to a crisis of disconnection and despair.

Finding a balance is crucial to combating the internal crisis of disconnection and despair and to creating space for hope to take root and grow. If we don't, social media will continue to be a social health issue rather than a platform for healthy social connections.

HOW WE SHOW UP: GUIDES FOR DIGITAL HABITS

This social shift to spending more time online has adjusted our habits; there's no doubt about that. So now we look to methods for restoring balance in our digital behavior patterns. Use the questions below to reflect on your own digital habits:

- Can I easily go hours and even days without being in online communities?
- When I am around other people, am I frequently looking at my phone?
- Do I post when I'm on social media, or am I doomscrolling through other people's content?
- After time in digital communities, do I feel more fulfilled, or do I feel restless or stressed?

Growing awareness about the harms of screen time and social media use is not meant to deter us from being online but rather to encourage us to expand our connections beyond a screen. If we discover an imbalance in our behavior patterns—hundreds of hours scrolling versus schoolwork, for example—we can always replace some of our digital habits with hope-based ones. When our interactions are meaningful rather than mindless, genuine connections grow.

Here are some suggestions to restore balance in our online behaviors:

- Keep away from the comparison game. In that game, everybody loses.
- Consume less; contribute more.
- Be present with people in person and selective with the moments you share online.
- If you wouldn't say it to someone's face, better not say it behind a screen.
- Prioritize connection over projecting perfection.
- Preset your intentions: mindless scrolling or meaningful interactions?
- Don't put all your eggs in one media basket. Gather content from different sources; the algorithm won't do it for you.
- Protect your privacy. Not everything needs to be public.

CREATING SPACE FOR HOPE

Throughout my career, I've witnessed how critical it is to create space for genuine human connection, not a space that is curated. As we've discovered, people are lonelier and more hopeless than ever. Yet they are also yearning for a space to really connect and cultivate hope.

This space isn't easy to find, but I've seen firsthand how it's simple to build. We start by allowing it to be a space without judgment. A space to feel like you're not the only one, and maybe there is a better way to deal with everything you're up against.

A space where you aren't the one with all the answers, giving everything to everyone except yourself.

A space where, in seeing others, you feel a surge of courage to let yourself be seen too.

A space to be broken or on the verge of breaking, and to have that be okay.

A space to show up with the heartbreak and hope you carry.

A space that is here for it all.

A space that is *here* for all of *you*.

Providing this space is what The Five Habits of Hope is about. My hope is that if you're ready, you'll turn the page and create space for hope.

WHEN OUR INTERACTIONS ARE MEANINGFUL RATHER THAN MINDLESS, GENUINE CONNECTIONS GROW.

FOUR

HEALTH AND HOPE

Now that we've discussed the social shift online and how it's impacting our connections and loneliness, contributing to our health, and causing us harm, let's examine the connection between health and hope. We'll break down how hope shapes our lives and why it holds so much significance.

A FORMULA FOR HOPE

We use the word *hope* every day in our culture: "I hope you feel better" or "I hope I get the job." But even though it's a common word, it has not always been well understood, especially in its connection to public health.

One definition of *hope* is a "desire accompanied by confident expectation or belief,"[1] while another describes hope as the willpower to change and the willpower to bring about that change.[2] Both definitions emphasize that hope comes out of a yearning and leads to a pursuit.

Psychologist Rick Snyder determined that hope involves two key components: pathways and agency.[3] He explained that hope requires having a clear goal, identifying pathways to achieve that goal, and cultivating the agency—or willpower—to pursue it. In order to help combat the growing internal crisis in society, we'll break down this process in a similar way but with a little twist. Our hope formula will look like this:

(DRIVE + DESTINATION) X WORTH

Here, we can see that hope requires ambition ("drive"), a path for taking action ("destination"), and belief in our inherent value ("worth"). In our application of Snyder's process of hope, we're adding self-worth to the equation. The more we build habits to value our own self-worth, the more hope increases, and the more healing feels within reach. You'll see that instead of a "+" for worth, I'm using an "x" because it's that important—worth has the power to multiply hope, causing exponential impact.

Knowing you are worthy enough to take action is foundational. It's kind of like if I have a goal to race in a marathon. I'm excited to try to be optimistic about the training. I have a plan to lace up my sneakers and hit the ground running, and I feel motivated to execute my plan. But what happens when I scroll on Instagram and see a friend who is training with a personal trainer? Now I'm intimidated and don't think I can do it anymore. I shut down. My confidence has escaped with comparison because I didn't know my inherent worth. Self-doubt talks me out of taking action.

For me to race in a marathon, I need more than ambition and a destination. I need to believe I belong in that race too, even if I don't have a personal trainer. I need to know that I am enough, just as I am. Belief in my intrinsic value will help make habits sustainable because they are attached to something beyond just a feeling. A sense of self-worth gives hope a stable foundation to hold on to.

By combining these essential elements—*(drive + destination) x worth*—we create a new value system that includes how we see ourselves in the equation. We understand hope as a deliberate and personal exchange. Hope can help us out of self-doubt, but not without us choosing to combat the fear with belief in our inherent value first. It also requires effort on our part. Being passive or sitting on the sidelines won't cut it. Hope is formed through action, grounded in our beliefs, and maintained by our involvement.

Hope is not free; it comes at a cost.

THE COST OF HOPE

When we hear *costs*, we usually think in financial terms. And while hope is an investment, when it comes to our internal journey, the exchange is an internal one too. Hope requires effort and commitment to the process, which can be a scary feat for anyone. For some, hope costs pride and comfort. For others, it requires courage to trust and the boldness to partner beliefs with action.

Ultimately, hope requires sacrifice. We must let go in order to let in.

What do we need to let go of? In the hope exchange, we need to let go of fear, doubt, and control—so that we can let in faith, self-worth, and surrender.

- By letting go of *fear*, we can have the *faith* that hope requires.
- By letting go of the *doubt* that consumes us, we can choose to believe that we are *worthy* of hope.
- By letting go of *control*, we can *surrender* the process and receive what we hope for.

HOPE EXCHANGE

FAITH > FEAR

DOUBT > SELF-WORTH

CONTROL > SURRENDER

Without this surrender of fear, doubt, and control, we'll go back to our old habits and the patterns that keep us stuck. Hope will continue to feel fleeting—soothing in one moment and gone with the wind the next. This exchange is a vital investment in building habits of hope.

As with any investment—time, energy, finances, education, whatever it may be—our sacrifices show what matters most to us. An internal investment is no different. It confirms we value ourselves and that we are worth investing in. Think back to our formula of hope if you need a reminder: *(drive + destination) x worth.* Too often, we pour out ourselves for those around us with little room left to invest in ourselves. Or we are simply unaware of our own inherent worth. We need a foundation of self-worth to give hope something strong enough to hold on to.

SCIENCE SAYS: HEALTH AND HOPE

I didn't always appreciate the connection between health and hope. It didn't seem like something you could study or measure. How could it be something to count on or to trust?

In modern Western society, we're taught everything from history to science, mathematics, and the fundamentals of physical health, yet navigating our emotional well-being is largely overlooked. While the topic of mental health has edged into mainstream culture over the years, it's still a widely taboo subject for a lot of people. Even so, developing language to talk about such important topics is a skill that we can learn, a process guided by habits.

Researchers in psychology, neuroscience, and medicine have been uncovering hope's crucial role in mental health. In fact, hope is found to be the single greatest predictor of physical, spiritual, and mental well-being.[4] While lacking hope hurts, having hope heals.

In earlier chapters, we discussed the growing surge of anxiety, depression, and substance abuse. It turns out hope has proven to be a key factor in promoting recovery for each of them and more. Social scientists continue to find that people with higher levels of hope have a greater ability to manage anxiety, stress, depression, and other mental health issues.[5] The benefits don't stop there. Someone with high hopes will deal better with trauma as opposed to those with lower levels of hope. This doesn't mean hope solves trauma, but it does aid in the healing process.

When we cultivate hope, we feel more secure in taking the next step toward our goals. It helps us find purpose and discover new ways to regulate emotions. As a result, if we have more hope in our lives, we'll be more likely to stick to healthy habits, which will impact how we think about the future and our success in it. Take our performances in the classroom and workplace. Hope has been shown to lead to a 12 percent gain in academic performance for a student, and more hopeful employees reach their quarterly goals more often in the workplace than those who have low levels of hope.[6] Hope-based habits build pathways for success.

Despite what I initially thought, hope is more than just a fleeting feeling; it's a cognitive process—and a science. Scientists have even introduced the concept of "hope molecules," showing that physical activity can trigger the release of these hope molecule proteins in our bodies. When these hope molecules are released, they have been linked to reducing inflammation, easing anxiety, and boosting mood and mental health.[7] This demonstrates how moving our bodies can create biochemical changes, generating feelings of hope. Kind of makes me want to get up right now and get moving.

If all these links between hope and health weren't convincing enough, there are more benefits to consider. In life-and-death situations, hope is a protective factor that can directly impact the outcome of our choices while in an internal crisis. In clinical settings, promoting hope is central to building interventions for anyone experiencing thoughts of suicide.[8]

I learned this firsthand while building and running a crisis text line. Whenever a person texting the line was experiencing distress, I'd ask them to describe something or someone that brought them hope, and they would feel better about their situation. In many instances, having something to be hopeful for was why they chose to keep living.

Hope is a driving force behind day-to-day behavioral change, ultimately supporting our journeys in habit formation. Now that we know how powerful hope can be for our health, we might wonder how habits play into all this.

THE IMPORTANCE OF HABITS

I used to think that changing my habits was such a burden and would make my life boring or less fun. I needed to change my eating habits. Stop my reality TV binging habits. Develop workout habits. Yeah, yeah, yeah. It all felt daunting, antagonizing, and the mere thought of breaking bad habits and creating good habits was exhausting.

Thankfully, in recent decades, habits have been the center of personal growth and cultural conversations. The groundbreaking work of psychologists, neuroscientists, thought leaders, and social scientists has shown how breaking down habits into small, digestible bites has a lasting impact. James Clear described habits in his book *Atomic Habits* as "small, consistent actions that, over time, create significant personal transformation."[9] In other words, tiny improvements can lead to long-term success.

Knowing this, we can approach building habits as minor adjustments rather than climbing Mount Everest on day one of our adventure. Such a relief!

There's more good news. Studies show that habits significantly impact our mental health. When we repeat a healthy habit enough, we can alter previous behavior patterns, improving our mood in the process. Author and psychotherapist Richard O'Connor simplified this by saying that the more we practice good habits, the more our brains will grow and change in response, making habits easier.[10] Another way to think of this is that habits speak to our minds and influence our hearts to take action. If we are experiencing anxiety, for example, established daily habits ground us, offering a sense of stability in our routine practices. Routines are refreshing for our souls, inspiring a sense of order in which we find comfort.

Consistency is the key to building mental health habits, so it is recommended that behavior adjustments be small. The goal is to identify what we can do within our control and then take small steps to replace old patterns we feel trapped by.

INTERNAL HABITS

Internal habits are emotional patterns. They shape how we perceive ourselves, others, the world, and our situations. These internal habits manifest through our emotional processes, influencing how we respond, regulate, and react to the world around us.

Internal habits, like hope, also impact our health. If we have healthy emotional habits, these routines help reroute feelings from the inside out.

Our brains are highly malleable, and they can actually reshape neural pathways. When this rewiring happens, hopeful thoughts can influence our emotions. This is a process called *neuroplasticity*, the brain's capability to constantly rewire with every action, experience, and thought.[11] This means that if we stay in a pattern of behavior long enough, we can influence our emotional state—there can be a way out of how we feel.

If you've ever learned a new skill, you have experience with this already. The more you practice a sport or instrument, the more efficient your brain pathways become. Internal habits are similar. Take a response to stress for instance. If you shut down emotionally when you are stressed, this response becomes your brain's default pathway. By practicing a healthier outlet for your stress, like working out, you can actually sculpt new circuits in your brain, reshaping neural pathways.

Building a process for hardships—internal habits—is an indispensable tool kit for life. These habits are proven to reduce stress, improve emotional regulation, and promote resilience.[12]

Knowing this, we can use habits to our benefit, reshaping neural pathways into pathways toward our goals. As we do, the foundation of our thoughts and actions guides us through times when we are tired, run-down, overwhelmed, and stressed-out.

Consider public speaking for a moment. For many, public speaking is at the top of their greatest fears list. But let's stretch our imagination a bit—envision yourself speaking confidently in front of a large audience of people. Now, let's examine our internal habits by relating them to our senses onstage: what we hear, see, and feel.

- *Hearing:* The self-talk in our minds—the quiet whispers or loud critics—sets the tone for our internal habits. Sometimes, our inner voice is harsh: *They are going to hate me.* This negative self-talk traps our self-worth in a cycle of negativity and affects our mental health. But healthier self-talk—such as, *I am prepared and ready to share my talent*—reaffirms our values, empowering us to act toward our goals and step onto that stage confidently and passionately.

- *Seeing:* When our perspective is distorted, it limits how we see ourselves, others, and the world. When the curtain lifts, the lights above can either illuminate or distort our perspective. We may look out into the crowd and become intimidated by what we see. We may think we're all so different. When our perspective widens, we can see we are all in this together, and our differences are what help us make a difference. This is when courage and connection emerge.
- *Feeling:* Right before our introduction, our feelings come into full force. We may experience a rush of nerves or sheer terror before beginning the first part of our message; these feelings steer our internal habits. This is when our emotional response takes over. As we gaze out at the crowd of thousands waiting for our words, does fear pull us back behind the curtain, or does it drive us to deliver the presentation of our lives?

Internal habits run the show beneath the surface—the emotional patterns we can't see. The more we become aware of our self-talk, our perspectives, and our feelings, the more we can redirect our current patterns toward hope. Neuroplasticity allows us to reshape these internal habits. Each time we practice healthier self-talk, have an open mind, or channel feelings like fear into courage, we carve out new neural pathways.

Internal habits are the emotional processes that either pave the way for or block our paths to hope. The more we recognize them, the more power we have to reshape, redirect, or reconstruct them, and the more we can cultivate hope.

HOPELESS HABITS

We won't always feel like implementing hope-based habits into our lives; there will be plenty of off days ahead. There may even be times we feel hopeless about hope. Habits of hopelessness—such as ruminating on failures, avoiding challenges, and engaging in negative self-talk—can flood our minds with doubt and negativity, making us feel stuck. After being in this position long enough, hopelessness becomes more than a passing feeling; it grows into a cycle that traps us.

Research shows that replaying our past mistakes over and over, focusing on what went wrong, doesn't just make us feel worse—it actually blocks our ability to solve problems and find a way forward.[13] We can reinforce feelings of hopelessness when we constantly tell ourselves we're not good enough or things will never change.[14] If similar thoughts set in for you, don't forget the power of the brain in rebuilding neural pathways. We don't have to stay stuck; there is a way through.

When you're unsure how to keep going through another round with discouragement, try implementing a habit of hope, which you'll discover next. For example, prompt yourself with the following question: "What do I need?" A person who can support you may come to mind, and already you are empowering new emotional patterns to grow.

Hope is not just found; it's fought for and fortified. Just as a boxer will retreat to their corner of the ring in between rounds to regroup and recuperate, we must step away from what we're going through to recover. We can also recover our cognitive resources—our brain power—when we psychologically detach from stressful situations.[15] This means, in the critical moments when we want to quit, we don't just get back in the ring, arms flailing. We take a moment in our corner to recoup and reload some mental stamina.

When we take space for ourselves during difficult times, we form new pathways in our minds, expanding our options. We need these spaces to check in, recover, and then reengage. In this critical pause between battles, when we feel stuck or disheartened, these habits of hope step in, restoring hope for the next move.

Through preparation and recovery, we can step back into our circumstances with renewed strength and a sense of what's possible!

So, if you're ready, let me introduce The Five Habits of Hope.

HOPE IS NOT
JUST FOUND; IT'S
FOUGHT FOR AND
FORTIFIED.

FIVE

INTRODUCING THE FIVE HABITS OF HOPE

In my profession, I am constantly driving through new cities and small towns. Once I get to an airport, I typically rent a vehicle and then hit the road toward my next speaking event. Whether it is miles of pure farmland ahead or elevated rocky mountain terrain, I would be lost without Google Maps guiding my every turn—step-by-step.

Think of The Five Habits of Hope as a framework for your internal GPS. They suggest routes for navigating struggles as you move toward healing and hope. Occasionally, they will show caution warnings, potential detours, and roadblock signs in the form of hope blocks, which get in your way. Their goal is to serve as a guide for navigating your emotional world and building mental health habits for processing your feelings through reflecting, risk-taking, releasing, receiving, and repurposing.

What follows is an overview of each habit to survey your emotional landscape. In part 2, we'll dive deeper into each habit and give you space to engage.

THE 5 HABITS OF HOPE

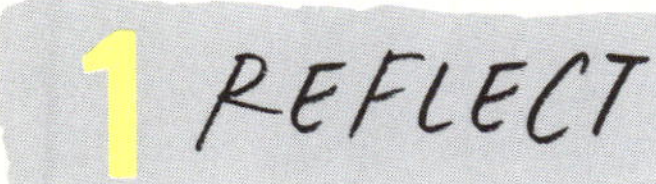

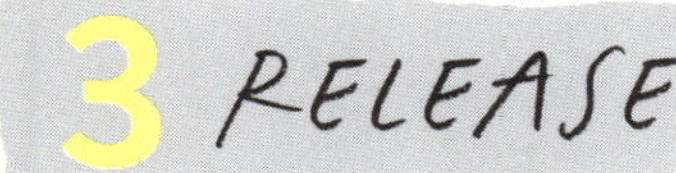

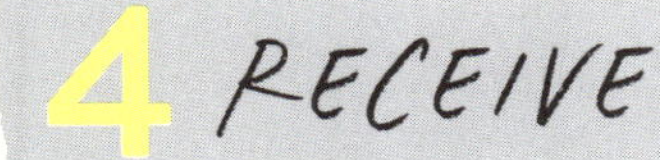

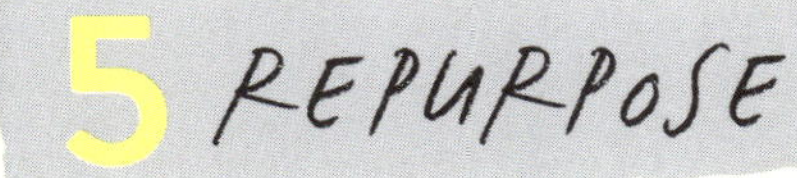

THE FIVE HABITS OF HOPE

1. Reflect

Before doing anything else, let's pause and check in. Reflecting is about glancing back at the footprints that have marked the journey before us, showing us how far we've come. As we pause and reflect, we are taking time to consider the struggles we've been through and the strengths we've gained along the way. It's not about getting stuck in the past; it's about appreciating where we've been so that we can best prepare for where we're going.

After delivering a keynote address at a leadership conference in California, I was packing up my materials when a staff member from the venue, who was not part of the audience, approached me to shake my hand. He said, "I didn't even know how much I was holding in until I saw so many people opening up about their struggles." His reaction communicated that even though he didn't participate in the exercises, he was still impacted by being in the room and watching others do so. It created a moment for him to look at his own life, and he was able to make space in his mind to start practicing the first habit: reflection.

Pausing to reflect may seem simple, but you might be surprised at how many of us are like that employee. We seldom pause and reflect. Living in a fast-paced culture does not help with this either. It doesn't always feel like there are enough hours in the week to squeeze reflection in. Some days, I am struggling with the basics:

eating, sleeping, and showering. Several times, I've even left the house with clothing inside out or my son pointing to my feet and asking, "Mom, why are you wearing pajama slippers instead of shoes?"

One key reason we don't always take time to reflect on our struggles is that we don't make space for it in our daily lives. This doesn't mean we don't care about our mental wellness; it's about the capacity to include it. For me, when I realized the repercussions of *not* making this space to reflect and the cost to myself of suppressing my emotions, I began to include this daily habit of reflection. I focus on thoughts, memories, and even struggles. It can sound like *Who am I grateful for? What situations did I once struggle with that I have now overcome?* The key is recognizing reflection isn't a step back—it's a way of looking back in order to move forward.

2. Risk

Once we've reflected on our emotional landscapes, then we can work toward taking emotional risks. These types of risks are not about chasing an adrenaline rush but instead focusing on our personal growth and relationships. They require vulnerability and courage to invest in what we care about.

The second habit, risk, may be the scariest one to take on, but it can also be the most rewarding. We take external risks all the time: It's a risk to leave your house on any given day, to be vulnerable with a friend, or to follow a dream. Similarly, it's a risk to stay isolated, suppress emotions, or hold back our deepest desires to pursue our passions. With these, we risk something even greater: never knowing what we're truly capable of. Both types of risk stem from a similar fear, but the outcomes are different.

If we were to look at why we don't take emotional risks, we'd discover fear at the center. Facing our fears and taking time to consider all the outcomes (not only the fear-based ones but the faith-filled desires as well) become the goal.

It's okay if we're not ready to be risk-takers right now. Remember, it's crucial to lean on your support systems whenever you need them. But when you are willing, taking risks can help you break out of your comfort zone and discover more of what you're capable of. Just as you won't land a job you don't apply for, you won't be able to fully heal from your struggles if you don't take some emotional risks.

We can't avoid the hazards that may come with risks, but we can learn to manage them by practicing this habit. Taking risks allows us to overcome fears and open up new opportunities for hope.

3. Release

After reflecting and opening yourself up to emotional risks, it's important to build the habit of release. With this habit, we are letting go of what no longer serves us in a healthy way—whether it's self-doubt, crippling fear, or the need for control. It's about creating space for genuine self-expression, stronger connection, and the pursuit of new possibilities.

The first time I was asked to perform spoken-word poetry, I

was tempted to resist—to withhold the words and keep them safely on the page. When I garnered the courage to speak them out loud, I experienced an emotional release, unlike anything I'd ever known before. It was extremely discomforting at first because I had been so used to holding back my words from the world. The truth is, if it were easy, it wouldn't have demanded the habit of release. This form of letting go is rare because, with it, expression is essential.

Consider a beloved music artist you listen to; you appreciate their songs because they released their work through self-expression in the first place. Yet, at some point, even they had to face the tension of holding back or letting their lyrics go.

When I facilitate The Five Habits of Hope with audiences, the most common sentiment I hear from participants who have "let go" of their emotions is a profound release. Withholding can be limiting, whereas the habit of releasing can be liberating. In releasing, we recognize we have a need, a desire, a will to let go in the first place. Finding a way to release the pressure, negative self-talk, and bottled-up emotions can open up a new channel for joy and hope. Whether it's an action we take or emotions we express through a song, letting go can be terrifying but also worthwhile. Releasing ideas, emotions, or burdens can open up pathways to mental space for healthy habits to flourish.

4. Receive

Have you ever struggled to receive a compliment? If so, you're not alone. The fourth habit, receiving, may require a little more practice. Whether we are receiving support, love, or hope, it positions us to confront how we see ourselves and our own self-worth. In doing so, we may recognize we have established a habit of staying silent about things that matter to us out of fear of not being deserving or because of shame. While releasing is about letting go, the habit of receiving is about letting in.

To approach this habit, we'll consider how we view our self-worth and whether we feel valuable enough to receive something in the first place.

Take Mara, for example. She was struggling in her relationship with her boyfriend. It turned out she didn't believe she was worthy to be loved by anyone. It didn't matter how romantic or genuine the gestures toward her were; she couldn't receive love in the way she wanted. After identifying this through reflection and then evaluating the risk of opening up to her boyfriend about what she was feeling, she made steps to confess her fears. In time, this release allowed for space in her heart to receive his love.

Growing in our self-worth isn't selfish, despite what our inner monologue might suggest. We aren't any less selfless when we accept support, encouragement, love, or even a compliment. Let me say that again in case you need another gentle reminder: Building self-worth is not selfish.

By practicing the habit of receiving, we get out of our own way, allowing ourselves to be seen, heard, and connected in the process. Receiving is one of the most powerful experiences we can have in building relationships and lives we are passionate about.

5. Repurpose

The fifth and final habit of hope is repurposing. With this habit, we focus on transformation and reframing thoughts and actions with intention. It challenges us to shift our perspectives, to see beyond the surface or the past, and to imagine possibilities through the lens of hope.

One of my close friends loves the environment more than anyone I've ever met. Her care and consideration for recycling are driven by her deep concern for the world. She doesn't believe anything is a waste; in her eyes, just about everything can be repurposed. The final habit, repurposing, reminds me of this friend. It finds and creates worth where others may see waste.

When I was struggling through grief after a close family member passed away from a drug overdose, I found hope when my pain had a purpose. It didn't happen right away, but in time, growing in the habit of repurposing transformed my grief into a greater purpose. It helped me heal.

This habit invites us to find creative ways to repurpose any emotion—pain, anger, joy, gratitude, sadness. We view each emotion as neutral and add value to how it's lived out. Through this, we discover emotions aren't inherently bad. I am angry that drugs stole the life of someone I love. However, when I repurpose that anger, similar to the way my mother refurbishes furniture, the anger becomes constructive. The shift is going from "anger is bad" to "anger can help me build something good."

When the habit of repurposing is fueled by hope, it can

expand our stories beyond chapters we once believed were finished. The end becomes a place where we can begin again, so long as we see value and purpose in it. Repurposing keeps hope alive.

THE FEELING FRAMEWORK

Now that we have laid the foundation for The Five Habits of Hope, we will integrate them into a five-prompt Feeling Framework. These prompts will help us practice each habit.

As we've discovered, hope often comes down to a feeling—we know when we have it and when we don't. Therefore, I paired each habit with a writing prompt to help us navigate our feelings. By integrating these emotional systems, which I call Feeling Frameworks, we can break unhelpful emotional cycles and replace them with more purposeful ones.

When we are ready, these prompts allow us to build processes to unpack our current emotional patterns. By making space for this practice, we start to see that our feelings, no matter how overwhelming, don't have to control us. Instead, we can use these tools to gain agency and carve out a path toward hope. The more we engage with each prompt, the more we break down the barriers blocking our way forward.

If any of this feels intimidating or you're not ready to dive into a prompt, that's completely okay. There is no rush. This is your journey; it's personal, and only you can set the pace. Remember, the process is just that—a process. Take courage from the stories shared by others throughout the book. Seeing how others have navigated these prompts might provide guidance and comfort as you begin your practice.

When I facilitate these exercises at my speaking events, people often see their peers responding alongside them. Watching others open up helps to normalize the experience, breaking down barriers of fear and hesitation. Witnessing it is powerful because it shows us that we're not alone in our struggles. The more we see others sharing their vulnerabilities, the easier it becomes to take that first step ourselves.

This book organizes each of the prompts in the same way I would facilitate them in person. While they are presented in a specific order, you can practice them in any sequence, depending on where you are in your journey. Consider the five prompts, which can be completed in as quickly as five minutes. They encourage the formation of a mental health habit centered around hope. The goal is, when you are experiencing a difficult time, to find a space within your day to engage with this practice.

1. *Reflect:* "I was struggling because . . ."
2. *Risk:* "I felt . . ."
3. *Release:* "I needed . . ."
4. *Receive:* "I stayed silent because . . ."
5. *Repurpose:* "I am hopeful for . . ."

1. I was struggling because . . .

The first prompt invites you to recall a time when you struggled and chose to remain silent about it. You can choose anything, an instance from ten years ago or two days ago. The goal is to be honest in your reflection. Don't overthink it.

Here are reflections to consider:

- A situation or a circumstance
- A pressure, expectation, or worry
- A relationship or feeling

2. I felt . . .

The second prompt challenges us to take an internal risk and explore our emotions honestly and directly. Naming an emotion encourages us to be real with what we are experiencing. It can be helpful to describe different senses you feel or list specific words that come to mind. Remember, you can pause at any moment. If you recognize you are not ready to reflect on a feeling, that is okay. It's a process. Be gentle with yourself and seek out your support system whenever you need it.

Thoughts to consider when approaching a feeling:

- Being real with how you feel helps you to heal.
- Use your senses to express details if you can.
- Choose as many words as you need, and don't feel pressure to share this with anyone.

3. I needed . . .

The third prompt examines the tension that comes from holding emotions inside. When we identify our needs, we make room to express them and practice the habit of release. In order to let go, we have to identify our needs. I don't know about you, but I have always wrestled with this one. Imagine what support in an ideal scenario would look like for you; the more detailed you can be, the better. Share names of people and specific actions you need to feel supported.

Questions to ask yourself when identifying a need:

- What would support look like?
- How would being supported feel?
- Do specific people come to mind who could offer support? If so, who?

4. I stayed silent because . . .

Prompt four is about uprooting our resistance to opening up; it's about letting in support and hope. We can't receive if we don't acknowledge why we stay silent and withhold. It encourages us to end the cycles that keep us struggling alone, beginning with "I stayed silent because . . ." In breaking this habit of holding back how we feel, we open up pathways for building patterns to process and heal. To do so, we can consider the pros and cons of keeping our struggles to ourselves. Will it hinder or help a situation or relationship?

Consider these questions when evaluating why you might keep your feelings hidden from others:

- Is it a belief system?
- Is it for another person?
- Is it because of a fear you have?

With this prompt, it may help to revisit the top three reasons others have shared as to why they don't open up about their struggles:

- "I don't want to be a burden."
- "I don't want to look weak."
- "No one cares."

5. I am hopeful for . . .

The fifth and final prompt empowers us to identify what we are hopeful for. For this one, individuals tend to identify a purpose beyond their own interests. Envision the faces of loved ones—a daughter, brother, mentor, friend. You can also think of beliefs you hold or ways you want to improve the lives of others. Ask yourself about the goals you have and what you are looking forward to. Are there accomplishments you'd like to achieve, experiences you want to have, faith you lean on, or causes you are willing to fight for? List as many things as you can.

Here are questions to consider when identifying what you are hopeful for:

- What are some areas of my life that I have hope for, even if they seem small?
- What are some situations I need hope in?
- Are there causes I care about or people I love who need hope?

To date, thousands of people across hundreds of cities have completed The Five Habits of Hope Feeling Framework. If you can't remember them all at once, that's okay. Focus on one at a time, as you need. If you would like to share them with others, print them for easy reference and display them in your classroom, in meeting rooms, or on your kitchen fridge.

Similar to how mental health professionals use emotional mood boards featuring animated expressions to help individuals identify their emotions, such as happiness, sadness, and discontentment, these five writing prompts guide us in practicing each habit of hope.

They serve as structured practices for recognizing and redirecting emotional habits. As we explore each habit, we learn it's a process to maintain hope. We refine our practice as we go.

MY FEELING FRAMEWORK

Here is an example of me completing the prompts about the loss of my cousin from a drug overdose:

1. "I was struggling because . . . I didn't know how to move on after he died. Life didn't make sense anymore."
2. "I felt . . . angry."
3. "I needed . . . to let go of my fear of being weak."
4. "I stayed silent because . . . I hated opening up about my feelings to anyone. I needed to receive support and know I wasn't alone."
5. "I am hopeful for . . . his joyful and playful spirit to live on through me and those who loved him."

YOU ARE NEVER ALONE

I struggled because I didn't think I was worth
it; my problems weren't big enough.
I felt worthless.
I needed love without pressure.
I didn't say anything because I
didn't want to be a burden.
I am hopeful for strength in myself.

I struggled with depression and self-harm.
I felt alone and hopeless.
I needed someone to recognize my need for help
and someone to talk to without feeling judged.
I am hopeful for better communicating
when I need help for my future.

I am struggling with pressure from work.
I was feeling overwhelmed.
I needed help with the workload.
I was silent because everyone had
their own responsibilities.
I am enough because I'm built for
this . . . the struggle doesn't win.

PART TWO

THE FIVE HABITS OF HOPE

SIX

HABIT #1: REFLECT

I struggled because I didn't believe in myself.

As we dive into the first habit of hope, let's start with an honest, anonymous reflection: "I struggled because I didn't believe in myself." Right from the start, we can sense that hope has enemies—intruders building barriers where belief could be. We might also discover how this type of reflection provides an intimate glimpse into a universal struggle: the emotional battles against self-doubt, fear, regret, or any obstacle taking the place of hope.

That's why our first stop on *The 5 Habits of Hope* journey encourages us to consider—and perhaps confront—these internal struggles: the ones that hold us back, hinder our potential, and undermine any half-hearted attempts to embrace hope. Otherwise, we might suppress these struggles or become so used to them that we question whether they can ever be overcome.

The habit of reflection is key to uprooting these internal conflicts. In order for hope to stand a chance against these barriers, we need first to acknowledge their presence. It's where this emotional processing begins. It's not easy work, but if you're ready to take it on, it's worth it. Let's dive in.

REFLECTERE

The word *reflection* comes from the Latin word *reflectere*, meaning "to bend back."[1] True to its origin, this is exactly what Habit #1 calls for: reflection. It encourages us to *reflectere*—to slow down long enough to bend back. By doing so, we are compelled to look inward.

It might seem counterintuitive that we need to look back in order to hold on to hope for our futures. If you're like me, with a mind that races a million miles an hour and is always trying to be productive, it can be difficult to slow down—let alone stop. This is especially true in our culture. In fact, nearly 80 percent of Americans feel overwhelmed by the constant expectation to be productive, which leaves little time for checking in on our emotional well-being.[2] As a result, our health and relationships can fall by the wayside.

Reflection involves cognitively acknowledging a process instead of avoiding it. Can you relate? Here are a few common reasons many of us resist reflection:

- We are constantly in motion, always on the go. There is a race for our attention, and our conscious minds are usually caught in someone else's agenda.
- We believe that if we were to stop whatever we are doing, our progress could also cease. Performance productivity can't afford that.

- We are afraid of what we will find. If we pause long enough, we may be terrified about where that present moment will bring us.

Pausing demands patience. If you're similar to me and prefer immediate results, patience is the last thing you want to practice. The hard truth is, it may never feel convenient to take a moment to consider the steep valleys we've barely survived or the daunting mountains still ahead. Without this pause, however, there is another cost—an emotional one. Reflection is connected to self-awareness, which is essential for emotional regulation and decision-making.

Without the habit of reflection, we risk speeding past emotional red lights, crashing into unresolved conflicts, or running on empty. While resting to reflect may not be the cultural norm in a society that awards productivity, it is essential in building habits of hope.

RED LIGHTS

Imagine leaving your neighborhood and approaching a traffic light blinking red—signaling not just to slow down but to come to a complete stop. Reflection is that red light. It serves as our emotional stoplight, signaling us to pause amid the competing distractions of our thoughts—the ones that persuade us to drive past struggles and detour around barriers of self-doubt or fear.

While we might prefer to pass unresolved issues and run over buried emotions, we can only go so far on a road without repairs. At full speed, it's only a matter of time before the wear and tear catches up with us. We can't maintain hope if we're running on fumes. The good news is that reflection can show us how to press the brakes. When we do, the habit of reflection creates space in our minds to assess, unpack, and intentionally map out how to move forward safely.

If I were to slow down and look in my own rearview mirror, I would see that the road behind me is full of potholes, faded paint lines, and cracked roadways. Sometimes, I purposely avoid this kind of reflection because I don't want to see it again. I'd rather not go there. If I do, I'm afraid of what I'll find.

Feelings of shame, for example, have been some of the most daunting to face. The more I refused to reflect on them, the larger the slits in my tires became. Eventually, I found myself driving on worn-down rims, barely moving at all.

Without reflection, we miss the signals that our struggles are trying to warn us about. When it comes to hope, we must practice this habit of reflection; otherwise, we risk being in constant motion, unable to notice whether our tires are wearing thin or the filters are clogged, causing the fuel pump to overheat again.

Understanding that the emotional practice of reflection is a visitation, not a destination, can be helpful. Reflection is a tool for growth, not a place to get stuck. It's a way of remembering what we may be trying to forget so it doesn't resurface at another inopportune time. Reflection enables us to revisit our struggles with purpose—not to pack up and live there.

We might not always be ready for reflection, though. We may want a friend or a professional support system to stand by us as we bend backward and look inward—someone who is ready to catch us if we lose our balance. Take your time to decide what strategy works best for you. This isn't a race. There are no winners or losers.

Be mindful that pausing to reflect isn't a common go-to pattern of behavior, and it's also not the easiest. If any of this feels uncomfortable or overwhelming, you're not alone. There's a reason this book is framed in emotional habits. They're not quick fixes; they require practice, time, and effort. Approach them with the same caution and care that you would extend to anyone you love who is learning something new. Allow room for growth and celebrate even the smallest step toward hope.

GREEN LIGHTS

For too long, I allowed memories to intimidate me, fearing the pain I'd feel if I confronted them. I didn't have another narrative besides going on my feeling detours to survive. I had no idea that I could shape my emotions so that they could be hopeful.

A captivating concept known as "constructed emotions" tells us our emotions are made, not triggered. This means we can reshape our emotions. Yes, you heard that right. We can reshape emotions and cultivate a sense of hopefulness. With this shift, reflection can be a green light, a way toward hope. The memories that surface as we practice the habit of reflection will serve as signals to the emotions we need to navigate through.

As we develop habits of reflection, we create opportunities for our conscious mind to engage with our emotional processing. When this happens, it allows us more say in how we experience and respond to what we've been through. Through this process, we can challenge unhelpful thoughts and reshape them into healthier ones. Reshaping emotions is linked to increased resilience in the face of challenges, decreased stress, and improved mental health outcomes, including reduced symptoms of anxiety and depression.[3] Similar to the way we develop any habit, the more we engage in this reflective practice, the easier it becomes.

The more we explore our experiences, the greater our likelihood of accessing rest stops along the way—places to take a break, recharge, and intentionally decide to reflect and build hope. By slowing down, we can identify negative thought patterns that need interruption and reframing, such as turning "I can't" into "I am capable" or "I failed" into "I will grow from this." Simply put, hope is not caused; it's created. It doesn't just happen to us; we get a say.

Even though we can't change our past experiences, we may be able to improve our relationship with them. We can allow emotions to be reshaped into forms that don't inflict pain every time we revisit them. The renewed shape that will form as a result may not be something we recognize or necessarily love, but at least the sharp edges will be mended enough to no longer cut at the slightest touch anymore.

This is why we look at the habit of reflection to build hope. It's a practice we can implement daily so that the next time we approach a red light, we aren't going from one hundred miles per hour to zero without notice. We are prepared for the stop-and-go, the pause-and-reflect habits that creating hope requires.

THE FEELING FRAMEWORK

In each of the habits, there will be a space for you to practice the Feeling Framework. Utilizing this framework helps to create intentional opportunities for practicing hopeful habits. It's a way to help hope become a habit, not just a fleeting emotion.

Here's how it works: Take a moment to complete the suggested prompt and make it a practice to do so whenever you find yourself up against any hardship. In doing so, you'll create more emotional space in your day-to-day and you'll build a behavioral pattern that cultivates hope.

What does that look like for me? If I were to personally respond to the first Feeling Framework that prompts me to reflect, I would say:

> I was struggling because . . . I didn't feel qualified. I didn't feel like I belonged.

This simple prompt is designed to kick-start your behavioral habits. Now you give it a try. Take a moment to think of a struggle that you've had difficulty opening up about. It can be a current challenge or something from your past. Pause, reflect, and then answer this prompt.

I was struggling because . . .

____

____

Reflection can be done in many different ways, from journaling to meditation, talk therapy, and more. We can also incorporate reflection in less structured ways, such as going for a run or while commuting to work. If I were to reflect right now on how I came to realize the power of reflection professionally, it would be when it stopped me in my tracks and redirected the trajectory of my life, eventually leading me here.

FROM DEFLECTION TO REFLECTION: MY FIRST SPEAKING EVENT

I had no idea what I was doing the first time I delivered a keynote speech. I was at a conference for detention officers, and the attendees were two to three times my age, experience, and education level.

My appearance probably didn't inspire confidence either. I walked in wearing knee-high boots, skinny jeans, and an oversized graphic T-shirt my friend had designed. If anything, the crowd seemed . . . annoyed.

I looked out at their crossed arms and downward gazes, suspecting they felt they were wasting their time on an inexperienced speaker trying to give a message of hope. Did I have something worthwhile to contribute? Even I wasn't sure. I was terrified. As the microphone passed to me, I looked out at hundreds of people staring blankly back. The indifference was crushing any confidence I thought I had.

I considered throwing the mic to the floor and making a quick dash to the nearest exit. *What am I even doing here?*

I imagined a million other places I could be as a twenty-one-year-old: a club, a friend's house, a concert, really anywhere but under harsh stage lights facing critics from an uninviting crowd. The microphone felt as heavy as my heart.

As I stood there, shame and self-doubt kept trying to take over. I wasn't sure how much longer I could handle the mounting pressure that was increasing my heart rate. I contemplated how much of my past I should share. Would revealing my experience in a rehabilitation program or my history of self-destructive behavior further discredit me in their eyes?

Up to that point, I'd been building up my résumé of self-destruction. Even though I had recently earned an undergraduate degree, my area of expertise had nothing to do with academia; it was in engaging in any activity that would spare me from facing my feelings, even at the expense of others. I defied reflection.

Though immediate family members had suffered lifelong health problems after being hit in a car by a drunk driver, I would dismiss their pain and drive intoxicated. Despite regular field trips to rehab centers and visits to family members who struggled with addictions, I'd deny it could ever affect me. At times, I had gone so far as to mix drugs with alcohol until I blacked out, an activity I first began in my early teens. After being raped during my freshman year of college, I felt poisoned. I no longer saw purpose in preserving or protecting myself. When people tried to offer support to me after I buried my cousin from an overdose, I was defensive and pushed them away. When it came to showing emotions, I was a master at deflection.

Before age twenty, I was already a professional at doing anything I could to prevent myself from experiencing what I feared most: feeling. If I did engage my feelings, there was a paralyzing fear of what I would find out about who I was and, even more, who I wasn't qualified to be. It went beyond imposter syndrome; it was internal oppression.

To overcome it, I needed more than self-help; I needed a process to navigate the deeply rooted oppressive thoughts I'd internalized over the years that told me I wasn't good enough or worthy. I had to acknowledge that I wasn't afraid of being disqualified only because of my past, but also because I was a young, biracial woman, and I'd never seen anyone with a similar background in the academic or professional settings I was in.

There was a lot for me to deal with, and reflecting gave me a moment to recognize what was really going on below the surface. By doing this, I could finally recognize the barriers that were blocking me from hope—the self-doubt and shame—and how they had been holding me back. Reflection didn't instantly resolve everything, but practicing it provided the clarity I needed to take my first steps toward healing and hope.

MY MOMENT OF REFLECTION

Reflecting began to shift everything for me, even as I was up there on that first stage. I may have been there to discuss inequity in the community I grew up in and share a message of hope, but little did I know I was the one who needed that message most.

Toward the end of my speech, I stopped reading my script, filled my lungs with as much air as they could hold, and took a chance to be honest about how I really felt. Memories of my cousin, who had died from an overdose, rushed to my mind. As I reflected on his life and senseless death, I realized I had been taking feeling detours to avoid processing it. Reflection helped me reshape the anger into anguish, revealing the deeper roots of my feelings.

As I proceeded to speak, a crack in my voice broke the death grip shame had on me, keeping my heart from opening up. There were tears building behind my eyes as the room fell silent. The only sound was the vibration from my suppressed fears, doubts, and control breaking free.

In real time, I was reflecting on painful memories—the very memories that ignited my soul to fight for hope and equity in the first place.

The more I reflected, the clearer my purpose as a speaker became. It refocused on what I was fighting for. I could finally envision the person I wanted to become in the next chapter of my life story. Reflection cleared the road ahead, making the path to hope within reach.

It was the pause I needed to shift the trajectory of my life. At that moment, I realized why I agreed to speak at that event in the first place: to be a voice for those I'd loved and lost, whose voices were silenced too soon. To advocate for the kind of second chances and mental wellness that countless others, like myself, were never afforded.

I did not know it then, but I realize now that I was speaking at this event because I was ready to face the darkness I'd endured head-on. No more feeling detours. I was finally confronting the divisive environment in which I grew up, surrounded by pervasive hatred over race and ethnicity. I opened my ears to hear the hateful language that used to crush my soul. I opened my eyes to face the version of myself I had tried to forget—the one who swallowed drugs, secretly wishing they would swallow me. I held the invisible scars left by unwanted hands after being assaulted. I embraced the void in my heart where those I loved—too many lives filled with potential—were reduced to memories after drugs, violence, or hopelessness stole them away.

In my lowest moments, I couldn't deny it: I wanted hope to be real. I was starting to feel like it was.

Right there, in front of an audience of strangers, I learned that hope is not for the faint of heart; it is something hard-earned. I admit

I was afraid, but the more I reflected, the more hope within me prevailed beyond pain or shame. That night on that stage was the first time my suppressed voice was set free.

As the speaking event concluded, the audience rose to their feet, one by one, and applauded. Our differences, so stark when I walked in, had disappeared.

That first keynote was a wake-up call. It forced me to choose whether or not I was really going to live out the message I was delivering. I realized after that day that if I was going to truly build a life I believed in fighting for, I couldn't continue to speed past my struggles. I needed to slow down, pay attention to the signs my feelings were showing me, and develop practices to process them.

Despair has been known to cast a looming, dark shadow over our lives, but hope has a way of illuminating the hidden parts of our stories, revealing paths that we didn't even know were there. Once we discover them, we can choose a new direction to take if we need to. Along the way, we may experience unexpected friendships, allies, or enemies within ourselves.

FEELING DETOURS: WHEN FEELINGS ARE NOT OUR FRIENDS

The best kind of friendships are built without judgment, yet I had turned my own inner world against me. It had become my worst enemy, judging everything about me. Slowing down, recognizing the flashing red stoplight ahead, and being willing to repair old thought patterns helped me reshape them into allies instead.

To nurture this healthier relationship with my feelings, I had to confront how much I had avoided seeing or hearing from them. Previously, my default reaction to any range of human emotion had been to do absolutely anything other than feel it. Instead, I preferred to deflect, dismiss, deny, defend, distract, and devalue my feelings.

These responses—what I came to call "feeling detours"—allowed me to suppress the emotions I couldn't control or understand. I grew to perfect this process from my youth to my teenage years and eventually into young adulthood, where it nearly stole my life. I preferred feeling detours because I didn't believe in hope. I thought hope was for happy, healthy, and holy people, not me.

When we acknowledge our own feeling detours, we can recognize whether we are falling into the trap of making our feelings the enemy. Can you relate to any of these examples of feeling detours?

- *Deflect:* Hopping, skipping, or running away in order to change courses and the conversation.
- *Dismiss:* Sending your feelings away as if they are not deserving of your attention.
- *Deny:* Refusing to grant your feelings a seat at the table.
- *Defend:* Building walls or shields to protect yourself from potential threats.
- *Distract:* "Checking out," the ultimate diversion.
- *Devalue:* Underestimating your self-worth.

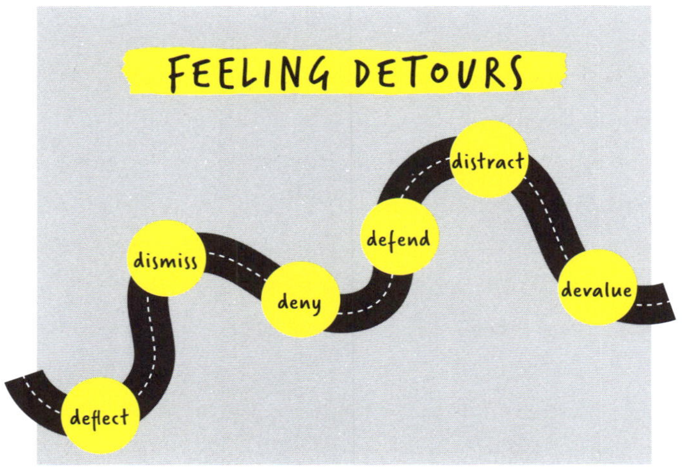

We may think we're avoiding emotions by going around them, but really, we end up right back where we started, in front of the same feeling again. Detours get us right back to the same road after all. Ignoring feelings won't make them disappear. And while our feelings may not feel like our friends, making them our enemies isn't the answer either.

To reflect on our feelings, we need to find a neutral, common ground—a place where they can be acknowledged, where we don't fight them, and where we can coexist with them. If we keep side-stepping our feelings—whether by deflecting, dismissing, denying, defending, distracting, or devaluing them—we become trapped in their endless loop. We take fewer risks. We feel less of what we desire. Our relationships become deprived of depth and connection. As noted in earlier chapters, feelings of disconnection and despair can trigger an internal crisis when we suppress our emotions for so long that we no longer have room to contain them.

So how do we turn things around? We look to hope as an antidote to our feeling detours and our internal crisis of disconnection and despair. Even more, we look to creating hope through emotional habits, such as the practice of reflection. We pause and consider the surrounding emotional landscape. Is there a barrier to hope in front of us?

Habit #1, reflection, lights the path ahead of us so that we can clearly see what is standing in our way toward hope. Whether we confront our fears of failure and reshape them into a list of courageous actions we are ready to take, or we recognize self-doubt and pinpoint areas of self-worth that require our focus, reflection acts as the green traffic light signaling us to take our first step.

Be on the lookout for when feeling detours try to tempt you back into their domain. Stay alert for their tactics that attempt to convince you: "It's no big deal; just pretend it never happened," "Toughen up; no one will care," or "Just suck it up and numb the pain."

Keep in mind that the best friendships—with others or yourself—aren't judgmental. They are built on honesty and communication.

THE MAP OF OUR MINDS

As we reroute from feeling detours toward hope, we can do so by giving language to our feelings so they don't feel as foreign or intimidating. There's nothing our suppressed struggles hate more than being seen. Pain and secrecy, after all, thrive in the dark.

Habit #1, reflecting, is not just a simple practice; it has the power to expose what's hidden and alter the course of our lives. For the next few moments, take time again to reflect as we pause and process the following questions:

- How could reflecting look in your daily life? List a few practices you could start today.
- Are you stuck in fear, living in a past relationship and bringing its residue into a current one?
- Is doubt in your qualifications and abilities keeping you stagnant, refusing to take risks in areas where you desire a change?
- Is your desire to control the outcome of something—perhaps an upcoming project or relationship—causing you to obsess over and micromanage what hasn't yet happened?
- Has a specific diagnosis or circumstance prevented you from seeing yourself as worthy and valuable? Have you become hopeless in it?

Developing a habit of reflection is the first step in the crucial process of building habits of hope. Any time you recognize you are about to deflect, dismiss, deny, defend, distract, or devalue your emotions, try finishing this sentence instead: "I am struggling because . . ." This way, your struggles don't get the chance to take root below the surface. When we take the first step of being honest about what we have been through or where we are right now, we get back on the highway of healing.

Awareness isn't the final answer; it's the first step. The habit of reflection acts as our guide, with red and green lights reminding us where our emotional habits may need attention and processing.

Reflection helps us to reshape the map of our minds, as tangled, complex, and troubled as they may seem. Pausing won't derail our progress; it resets and realigns our intentions so that we can move toward hope with confidence and clarity.

By prioritizing daily reflection and leaning in to Feeling Frameworks and prompts, we create space to practice. Before we realize it, we have developed the courage for the next stop on our journey of hope: the habit of taking risks.

YOU ARE NEVER ALONE

I struggled because I didn't think I had a right to not be OK.

I struggled with loss, self-doubt, and medical issues.

I was struggling because of the stress and anxiety of feeling alone.

I struggled because I put a smile on my face, but I hurt every single day.

I WAS STRUGGLING WITH MOVING ON.

SEVEN

HABIT #2: RISK

I felt helpless and weak . . .

Often, before experiencing a moment of bravery, there's an inner battle with our self-worth—a struggle that resonates with the note above: "I felt helpless and weak." The question becomes, Do we risk believing we're weak or worthy?

There is a phrase I hear often, nearly every week, and it usually comes after someone cries in front of me or shows any sign of vulnerability. Whether said by young children or older adults, from people in the Bronx, New York, to Austin, Texas, there are two words I almost always hear after someone expresses any emotion in front of me. I bet you can imagine by now what they are: "I'm sorry."

Apologizing after showing emotion is a common cultural response, something society has ingrained in us. How else do we explain the phenomenon of people across hundreds of cities and demographics having the same response? As a culture, we have normalized masking feelings so much—even more now, with filters on social media—that we apologize for being genuine. We apologize for being real about how we feel.

This apology is symptomatic of a larger societal issue: We see emotions as weakness, and we equate weakness with unworthiness. It's a social norm deeply embedded in a belief system. For example, we might think it's cowardly to cry in front of our family, because we may feel we're letting them down. We think we should be able to handle it all; it may even be unacceptable not to.

With this mentality, we develop and reinforce behaviors that withhold feelings for fear of looking weak or causing concern in those we care about. We decide to handle the hurt on our own so long as it doesn't cause hurt to the people we love. This leads to us toughening up and closing off emotionally—a pattern that blocks hope for deeper connection in our relationships.

If we'd like to break this inner habit, we need to replace it with a new one, our second habit in our healing journey: risk. When building a hope-based habit of risk-taking, I'm not referring to gambling or high-adrenaline activities. I'm referring to an emotional behavior pattern of taking risks. This may look like opening up vulnerably, being in love, or believing in an idea so much that you invest in it. And the risk comes in not knowing the outcome, which is scary. You risk potentially hurting someone, breaking societal norms, failing, being rejected, or being found as unworthy. You may be embarrassed, shamed, or misunderstood when you take emotional risks like this. On the other hand, you could receive a promotion, develop a new friendship, or be embraced by an entire community.

There's a risk no matter what.

This isn't to say being tough isn't necessary and healthy. I admit the "toughen up" mentality served me well as a former college athlete. When I was afraid of a competitor or wanted to skip an early morning workout, I reminded myself to toughen up, and I did.

Healthy toughness is about resilience, courage, and emotional regulation. It's about responding in a way that aligns with your values and self-worth. The difference is that one is constructive and the other can become self-destructive. Hope grows where a solid foundation of healthy resilience takes root.

TRUTH OR DARE?

Have you ever played the game Truth or Dare? It's a social game where participants take turns deciding whether to answer a personal question (truth) or perform a challenging, sometimes humiliating or dangerous activity (dare). It's interesting how someone would choose a dare over a truth. At times, facing a risky or even embarrassing task in a dare can feel more tolerable than being vulnerable, especially around peers.

As economist and educator Peter L. Bernstein wrote, "The word 'risk' derives from the early Italian *risicare*, which means 'to dare.'"[1] Ironically, telling the truth can feel like the ultimate challenge—the most difficult and *riskiest* dare of all.

Here are a few common reasons we may resist risks:

- ***Rejection:*** We'd rather stay quiet than risk being unaccepted for our ideas, passions, or identity.
- ***Being hurt:*** Yes, we are tough, but don't ask us to open up. That might hurt too much.

- ***Failure:*** Better yet, if we don't take risks, we won't have to dust ourselves off and try again.
- ***Being discovered as unworthy:*** Nothing could be worse than confirming our deepest insecurities. For those of us with low self-worth, the mere thought is unbearable.

Risks reject certainty; they take chances on change. If, like me, you prefer comfort over the unknown, then you won't want to put the habit of risk at the top of your priority list. It can even feel unnatural. Without emotional risks, however, there are other consequences to consider. Our comfort zone, for instance, will never be spacious enough for all our relationships and ideas to thrive. By design, it's a small, controlled area—where boundaries keep you confined or feeling isolated and alone.

Having hope is a risk. There's no way around it. The reality is that hope may not lead to the outcome we want; hope doesn't guarantee results. Without it, we'll never know what could have been if only we had dared to believe in our ideas, our feelings, and the life we truly wanted to create.

RESISTING RISK

Do you remember how our habits can create new pathways in our brains? If, year after year, we associate weakness with worthlessness and apologize for natural emotional releases, or if we stay isolated in our comfort zones instead of opening up, we start to shape our emotional response to vulnerability. After a while, we will say, "I'm sorry" or "I don't want to get close to anyone" without even realizing it. As an alternative, hope-based habits encourage us to process emotions rather than withhold them, allowing us to create more meaning in our lives. The more we foster an automatic response, like the habit of withholding emotions, the harder it becomes to break it. So be patient with yourself throughout the process.

Let's explore another way to break down common emotional responses:

1. We choose to **reveal** what we feel.
2. We choose to **conceal** what we feel.

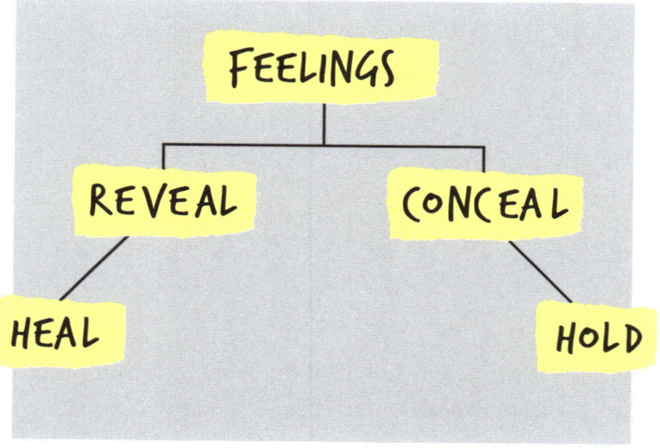

When we reveal emotions, we open up to those feelings, process them, and move toward healing. On the other hand, suppressing our emotions instead of processing them can become harmful.

Author Bessel van der Kolk illuminates this dynamic in *The Body Keeps the Score*,[2] a book about treating traumatic stress. In it, van der Kolk explains that our bodies are at war with themselves, holding on to suppressed emotions and overwhelming us with stress and other physical symptoms if those emotions are not addressed. This manifestation affects our overall health. Considering this, we can see how emotional suppression is not only a mental strain but also a physical one.

Picture a dam holding back water. If you keep filling the dam and don't manage the water levels, pressure builds. That dam is going to break. The emotions inside our bodies aren't much different. We have only so much space to contain our feelings before they burst out.

The problem with supressing feelings is that they will eventually have a hold on us. How can we navigate feelings if we don't even permit ourselves to experience them?

Suppression has nothing to do with being strong—it creates a ticking time bomb. It's only a matter of time before suppressed feelings find a way to break through the surface, just like that dam. Sooner or later, those pent-up emotions will find a way out.

THE FEELING FRAMEWORK

The second Feeling Framework prompt—"I felt . . ."—helps us implement this process. It's a way to confront any emotional response to resisting risk and to put language to a feeling. When we express our feelings, we break down the barriers between our inner worlds and external expressions. We refuse to remain in the same cyclical thought patterns that stop us from taking risks on what we value most.

Another benefit to articulating our emotions is that it helps regulate them. When we label emotions—similar to identifying ingredients on a food label—it triggers a chain of events in our brains. Picture two main "ingredients": one activates our emotional regulation (the right ventrolateral prefrontal cortex), while the other reduces activity in our emotional processing center (the amygdala).[3] Yes, we can decide what to eat without reading the food label, but knowing what's inside allows us to make more informed choices confidently.

If I were to practice this right now, I would say,

> I felt . . . exposed and afraid of what people would think when they read this.

Instead of allowing these internalized thoughts to loop on endless repeat, I interrupted them and risked being vulnerable. I labeled them and let them go. At first, I felt a wave of discomfort about doing so, but after I read it aloud to myself, I experienced a profound sense of relief. I had taken a risk to be real, and for better or worse, it felt good. My fears were no longer racing through my mind; they had found another space, apart from me, to exist.

If you're not in a place to take an emotional risk, that's perfectly okay. There's a reason so many people prefer to take a dare rather than speak a truth. Take your time. Replacing any habit has its challenges; the important thing is being on the best path for you. If you do feel ready to put the habit into practice, give it a try.

After reflecting on a struggle you were dealing with, consider how you felt about it.

I felt . . .

____

____

In the first habit, we explored the emotional detours we take to avoid reflection. With the habit of risk, we shift our focus inward, examine how we see ourselves—our self-worth—and choose to build a life of hope, if we dare.

THE TOUGH TEST

The best way to explain the practice of emotional risk-taking is through an exercise I use during my live events. If you're up for it, let's take my Tough Test together: "Raise your hand if you think you're tough."

I often ask this question to audiences at my speaking events. Immediately, arms rise all over the room. Next, I invite a volunteer to the stage for an exercise. I call it the "Tough Test." It's a fun activity for them to prove just how tough they really are in front of their peers, if they dare.

I don't define what being tough means before the activity begins. Instead, I invite the audience to define what toughness means to them personally. I offer a few examples of what shaped my own understanding of toughness, including personal and cultural factors.

If they choose to volunteer, their definition of toughness comes down to their perspective and beliefs. The only requirement for the Tough Test is believing you are tough. Spoiler alert: Every volunteer ends up associating toughness with being able to withhold emotions.

FISTS OUT, FEELINGS IN

As the activity begins, I invite the entire audience to participate in a portion of it from their seats. First, I ask, "If you've ever been through a really tough time, make two fists with your hands." Go ahead and try it yourself. Fists out, feelings in.

Next, I'll ask, "If you have been through a really tough time before and didn't tell anyone about it, squeeze your fists as tightly as you can." This might sound simple at first, but the rule is to keep your fists clenched for as long as possible (without bursting a vein, of course!). We're tough, remember?

Within minutes, I usually hear groans of discomfort from participants. I'll see bodies shake or hands turning pale. They look up at me, wondering if they can release their fists yet. I smile and assure them, "You've got this. You're tough! Keep going . . . if you can."

What we are demonstrating is a physical representation of what we do internally: white-knuckling emotions we wrestle within. Withholding feelings internally is not much different than holding a clenched fist physically. There's a tension—a fear of giving up if it means giving in. Showcasing how tough we are is not easy. It's work.

If we consider the energy it takes to maintain a fist forcefully closed, imagine how similar it must be to withhold feelings all the time. No matter how much we shake and struggle to clench our fists, it doesn't make what we feel go away. We can reflect on it or not. We can risk loosening our grip or stay closed up. Either way, our feelings don't go away simply because we don't acknowledge and express them.

STILL PROVING YOU'RE TOUGH?

Okay, if you've made it this far, still clenching your fists, incredible job! I invite you to release your hands and whatever you're holding on to now. Can you identify an immediate feeling you have when you release your clenched fists? The most common response I hear is "relief."

If you were to try to go about your day with your fists clenched—eating, giving a hug, driving—you would quickly feel the limitations you have. That's how it is with suppressed feelings. You may go years without acknowledging them, but there will be a cost. The expense is the effort you spend holding in and holding back. You may be able to function and build relationships, but it won't be at full capacity.

We won't experience real freedom without tools to navigate our feelings. They will, ultimately, have a hold on us. We can go from our teens to twenties and find our way to our sixties and beyond without ever releasing the hold that a previous tough experience had over us.

I learned this all too well in prison.

RISKING HOPE: A LIFE SENTENCE OR LIFE SAVED

It was a weekday afternoon when I got the call. There was a request for me to come and speak to incarcerated men in a Michigan state prison. Many were serving life sentences. Confused, I questioned if they had phoned the right person.

I shared that I had no prior experience in this area and they should probably find someone else. At the time, I had worked with youth in detention centers and women in transitional housing once they had already served their sentences, but not with men in prison. I doubted I had anything significant to offer them.

The organizer of the event didn't seem fazed in the least by my inexperience. He had heard about my work building a former initiative called The Rewrite Project, which recognized the power of restoration and believed everyone deserves the opportunity to reclaim their story. The organizer was eager for me to bring this mission to the men in prison and seemed convinced I could help. It took some persuading, but eventually, and reluctantly, I agreed.

I drove up to the heavily guarded penitentiary on a blisteringly cold and gray winter day. I was told to follow a strict wardrobe etiquette that included no heels, tight clothing, or jewelry. After security, I made my way through the yard outside, where I felt heavy gazes from hundreds of men coming from every direction. I glanced at the guards, one standing in front and another behind me, and considered asking them to take me back to the parking lot. I admit I was scared.

The next thing I knew, I was being ushered into a classroom area where the director introduced me. Everyone looked up in my direction and smiled with anticipation.

I was now supposed to fill the space with something helpful. I hadn't prepared anything to hand out or a PowerPoint to discuss. It was just me in a dimly lit room full of men I assumed I had no ability to relate to. I was in a foreign territory.

I didn't try to teach. Instead, I chose to listen, to create space for them just to feel free to be themselves, knowing very well they might not experience freedom in a traditional sense ever again. I looked around and took in the tattoos telling stories on their skin and the fine lines, symbols of time, forming around the corners of their eyes.

I thought about how tough it must be to survive in prison. I wondered if they cared to open up at all or if they, too, were like me and struggled with the tension of withholding feelings, especially in front of others—let alone a stranger. To find out if they were willing to take the space to open up, I began by asking them, "What does being tough mean to you?"

What followed still brings me to tears, just remembering. A man sitting beside me on my right, well over six feet tall, leaned back and stared up at the ceiling. His tone was muffled as he openly reflected on memories of unspeakable abuse from his father. He went on to say, "Men don't show feelings; we've gotta be tough to survive." Most of the room nodded in agreement and even went further, saying, "Yeah, we gotta be tough and provide too."

The avalanche had begun. It was a landslide of releasing suppressed feelings for the first time. They kept confessing, "I've never told anyone this."

By starting the session with time to reflect, I gave them an opportunity to risk opening up emotionally. Through a facilitated prompt, figurative chains around their conscious minds were unlocked. There was no big speech. It was just a question about what being tough meant to them.

As a response, they allowed themselves to risk what they never thought they were allowed to: putting words to their emotions and daring to share their struggles openly. As they did, they realized how being tough had shaped their decisions and lives. As each person spoke, more opened up, disclosing past pain they had endured and never dealt with before. Stories of violence when they were children. Stories of pain they themselves had caused. Feelings of shame so heavy they could barely lift their heads as the words poured out. It was as if their pent-up emotions had been serving life sentences even before they were behind bars.

WE ALL NEED AN OUTLET TO FEEL

By the end of the hour, only one person hadn't shared anything. He was sitting diagonally from me, looking away every time I tried to make eye contact. I felt compelled to reach out to him even though he clearly wasn't interested in participating. I grabbed my chair and moved it a few feet directly in front of him. I asked him what being tough meant to him. He looked at me like, *Is this chick for real?*

Then, looking around at the other men who were nodding yes in encouragement, he realized I was for real. I stayed patient while he gathered his thoughts and worked up something to say. Holding his gaze, I wanted him to know—whether he wanted me to or not—that I saw him.

My heart still breaks, recalling the risk he took as he shared details about a childhood spent in what I'd imagined only in horror films. He seemed completely emotionless while reflecting on it. Hardened in his heart and tone. When he was finished, I didn't move or speak. No one else tried to break the silence either. There was a comfort in the quietness.

After a few minutes passed, he began—slowly at first and then heavily—to cry. I didn't offer answers or say anything as a response. I continued to hold my position and let him know I could see him by the way I looked directly into his eyes. We weren't allowed to hug, but in that moment, it felt as if every one of us was hanging on to something so potent in the air that it was wrapping its arms around us.

THE RISK OF TAKING SPACE

That room, full of men who were mostly serving life sentences for crimes ranging from selling drugs to murder, was the last place on earth I thought I wanted to be. Yet there I was, sitting in a prison and not feeling so different from them. We were brought together by the stories shared and the feelings expressed. Some I could relate to. For others, who were attempting to reshape guilt, I felt compassion.

I was no longer afraid to be there. Rather, I was full of hope and could feel they were too. I didn't show up with a book of how-to tactics or even an agenda. Instead, I offered a framework to reflect (Habit #1) and to risk opening up (Habit #2). The most eye-opening part of the entire experience was their gratitude for the space to open up. It reminded me of an invaluable lesson: *We all need an outlet to feel.* The problem is, we lack opportunities to do so; there isn't always space we feel comfortable in, and because of this, there are consequences.

These men in particular expressed that they had never told anyone what they were struggling with because they didn't want to burden anyone with their problems. They thought being tough was more than a physical attribute—it was about withholding their emotions.

Taking a risk to open up and share what we've gone through will always be tough. Even the toughest among us find it difficult. If we are going to reckon with our past and still have hope for our future, the risk may be scary, but it also can create opportunities for more depth and meaning in our lives.

Those men didn't have to take the space I provided with an open mind or heart—no one ever has to. However, whether it's a one-on-one or large-group setting, I've continued to see similar risks being taken across every demographic I work with. It seems people want to experience genuine connection.

I saw inmates take emotional risks and build emotional courage at that prison. I believe they opened up because they were tired of proving they were always tough. I believe it's because they wanted to have hope again, even if that hope stayed behind bars. Thankfully, it didn't though. I feel it even now, writing this.

YOU ARE TOUGH ENOUGH TO RISK

If you have been through a tough time in your life, you are tough. You don't have to prove it. I'm going to repeat that in case it didn't simmer long enough the first time: You have survived tough things. You are already tough. You don't need to exhaust your energy proving it.

Instead, you can shift your efforts from clenching your fists and keeping feelings hidden into building a habitual process to have hope. Just like practicing a sport you love, you can practice taking an internal risk by picking up a pen and writing a gratitude list or opening your palms and taking the hand of a loved one. Maybe your risk is sharing your story or your current feelings with someone. Maybe it's pursuing a passion or a relationship. Build your expectation of what's possible!

In order to develop a habitual practice of emotional risk-taking, we have to ask ourselves, *What are we holding on to instead of hope?* As we identify these things, we are one step closer to breaking the habit of withholding and replacing it with the habit of honestly expressing our feelings. And hope without honesty isn't the kind of hope we want to hang on to anyway.

Be mindful that once we start to be honest and acknowledge that we have been through some really difficult things, it can be tempting to hold back again. To wear a mask. To fight off anyone who is attempting to be there for us, inviting us to fully be ourselves. If you feel this way, you're not alone. And there's no rush to take an emotional risk. Building emotional habits takes time.

If you'd like to practice now, let's pause and process these questions about risk:

- What is the risk really about?
- Are you afraid of potential rejection or of failing? Do you know where this fear stems from?

- Does culture make it difficult for you to express feelings without judgment? Why do you think that is?

As we practice the habit of taking emotional risks, we can expand our perspectives even more and reflect on the stories of others. In them, we might notice a theme. You can hear how important it is for people to believe they must be emotionally strong, even if it means they must suffer in silence. In their pursuit of strength, you can sense a deep tension. The tension is between being strong, often for others, at the expense of ourselves.

Can you relate? I know I can.

I struggled with Jonathan's death and the impact it had on all aspects of life. I felt powerless, hopeless, scared, angry.

I struggled with the loss of my mom,
my son's mental health issues.
I felt lost and confused, disappointed, hopeless.
I stayed silent because I was ashamed and hurt.

I struggled to believe because I needed to be the rock for others.
I was feeling like I couldn't show emotion and I was hurt and angry but needed to smile.

I stayed silent to be strong for my family.

I STAYED SILENT BECAUSE I HAD TO STAY STRONG AND TAKE CARE OF MY KID.

A LIFE WITHOUT RISK

In my own attempt to prove toughness, I kept everyone at a distance to avoid being hurt. I suppressed everything, even when it was killing me to do so. I wanted to appear independent and never rely on anyone for anything. Relying on someone was a risky investment, and I convinced myself it was too great to take.

As I went on to build a process to feel my emotions, I built habits that reshaped my response to vulnerability. Slowly but surely, I became more open to taking emotional risks. I ended up realizing that I didn't want a life without emotional risks. A life without risk means rejecting potential—potential relationships, business opportunities, community connections, and more.

I no longer wanted to reject my potential. I wanted to know what I was capable of and to form real, meaningful connections.

Of course, taking risks doesn't always work out. Not every relationship moves forward, and not every professional idea I pursue succeeds. The difference now is that I have an internal process to heal from the outcomes, regardless of whether they are successes or setbacks. I'm not attached to what happens. And now, I risk rejection and connection every day.

Without risk, we won't chase our dreams, fight for our marriages, create art, or develop a genuine love for who we are. In order to take any emotional risk, we must learn what's at stake. What if our resistance isn't as much about letting someone *in* as it is about letting something we've been holding in *out*? If we refuse to communicate feelings, for example, because we don't want to risk rejection, we may end up risking so much more, like the entire relationship.

Here are a few questions to consider about a life without risk:

- Is the person you are building a relationship with worth your emotional risk?
- Are there people in need of the services, solutions, and ideas you want to give? What happens if they don't receive them?
- Do the people you are choosing to be in relationships with deserve to know more about you? Do you expect them to share vulnerably with you?
- How can you expect someone to know you if you won't risk opening up enough in order to truly know yourself?

The greatest artists and innovators of all time share one thing in common: They took a risk. They risked rejection; they risked connection. If they hadn't, they would have risked something more: not bringing an important part of who they are into the world.

WORTH THE RISK

To take any emotional risk, start with this perspective shift: You are worthy, not weak. Yes, believing we are worthy is risky. We must believe we are worth the risk if we are to replace old emotional patterns with hope-based ones.

Shifting our perspective from proving we are tough to believing we are enough doesn't mean we give up working. In fact, it's the opposite. When you realize you are talented enough, loved enough, or resilient enough, you don't have to exhaust energy proving it. Instead, you can redirect that energy toward what you value most.

You are strong enough.

Smart enough.

Loved enough.

Always enough.

When doubt tries to hold you back, you can confidently take risks on your potential, your relationships, and your dreams. You can have hope for your life and your future!

Here are some steps to take toward this shift:

Step 1. Broaden your definitions of *toughness* and *weakness*. This takes pressure off proving your toughness. In doing so, we practice breaking the response of withholding our emotions.

Step 2. Take space. Similar to the way the men in the prison did, take space—verbally, through writing, or by another form of expression—to identify feelings and eventually share them with others.

Step 3. Shift how you see yourself. You are not weak but worthy. The more you try to change your perspective in this area, the greater the chance you will believe it.

When we embrace the habit of risk, we don't feel compelled to apologize for expressing natural emotion if we need to. We hone and honor our worth. We practice perspective shifts. We take back the power to label our emotions and share our stories when we're ready. We do so, knowing there will be uncertainty and risk.

PERSPECTIVE SHIFT

The hardest work becomes internal. We are the quickest to judge ourselves unfairly and then to sentence ourselves to a lifetime of punishment. Our greatest offense is not believing we are worthy.

Here are some potential perspective shifts to consider:

- "I struggle with anxiety, so I can't do it." versus "I will consider ways to navigate my anxiety as I make choices and control what I can."
- "I am just an introvert; it's who I am." versus "I am more than one personality characteristic. I am capable of developing in different areas."
- "They broke my heart. I will never trust again." versus "My heart is shaped differently now, and the place it was broken has created more space to be filled by a healthy relationship (maybe even the one I have with myself)."
- "I am a victim. They stole my story." versus "I am a survivor, and no one can silence my voice or keep me from rewriting my story."
- "I need to be tough." versus "I am tough, so I don't have to exhaust myself in proving it. I am enough, and that is enough."

As we continue to shift our perspectives, we can see how feelings aren't all bad. Even anger and anxiety have their place in protecting or propelling us in healthy ways. We don't need to eliminate them but find ways to manage and express them.

The goal isn't to get rid of feelings but rather to gain tools to navigate them. We can do this by reengaging our perspective through the lens of hope: believing we are worth the risk of having hope in ourselves, our relationships, and our futures. In order to do so, however, we have to hold on to hope more than we hold our clenched fists.

The next time you're asked if you think you're tough, remember that true strength is defined by your own story. If you have an opportunity to open up, take that risk, embrace your worth, and get ready for a powerful release (Habit #3).

YOU ARE NEVER ALONE

I felt depressed and sad about my family.
I AM ENOUGH because I work
to be a better person.

I felt like a huge failure and
wanted to give up.
I am enough because I am
determined to help others.

I felt like a burden.
I am enough because I am
here and I am alive.

I felt isolated and depressed.
I am enough because I have been redeemed. I
have a purpose. I'm a support to my family and
friends, I am a wise person, I have been gifted.

EIGHT

HABIT #3: RELEASE

I needed support.

The first time someone tried to read something vulnerable I had written, I nearly had a panic attack. A close friend had spontaneously jumped in the passenger seat of my car and noticed my journal of poetry on the seat. They grabbed it to move it aside, but then curiosity invited them to crack open the cover and ask, "What's this?"

When they did, it was as if the air in my lungs had escaped my body. I was trembling for words, but nothing was coming out. I'm guessing the color drained from my face, and my eyes practically popped out of my head because my friend caught on pretty quickly —I did *not* want them to open it. They kindly put it in the back seat and then looked over at me again. "You okay?" they asked.

I wasn't. I may have lied and said I was, but I definitely was not okay. At first, I thought it was because I didn't want them to see my writing. To see *me* in that way. But after sitting with them in the car over the next hour, I realized something I didn't anticipate: I did, in fact, want that side of me to be known by them.

I was ready to share my scars through poetry, to introduce a side of me that didn't hold back what I felt. This side of me was brave and bold. Even though I was still getting to know this version of myself, I wanted to invite others into the journey. The more I considered it, the more I realized my panic toward my friend had come out of habit. Hiding was what I knew how to do; it's what I had always done. Releasing was something I needed to learn.

This brings us to our third habit of hope: release. When we build a hope-based habit of releasing, we are letting go of anything that is tipping us toward an imbalanced emotional state. This may look like pent-up energy or suppressed emotions or, in my case, panic over being vulnerable. When we practice the habit of releasing, we deal with these emotions by letting go, giving something away, or sharing a piece of ourselves. When I started sharing my poetry out loud, I was able to release a lifetime of suppressed emotions and was finally able to breathe. Once we release, we let go of the outcome and experience emotional freedom.

RELAX ALREADY

I currently have two incredibly thoughtful but unused gift certificates for massages. They are both fully paid invitations to "relax," yet I still struggle to prioritize doing it.

The word *release* means "let go," "set free," or "relax."[1] For me, the concept of relaxing resonates the most because I know I need it. The tricky part is, relaxing isn't natural for me; I have to intentionally build practices to master it. At some point, I have to acknowledge the aches in my lower back and the strains in my shoulders and say, "You know what? I need to make time for my massage already!"

Funny enough, releasing—much like relaxing—is not only beneficial for the soul but also great for the body and mind. When we let ourselves relax—both physically and mentally—we create space to release thoughts, tensions, ideas, and anything in our minds that needs air to breathe. My husband calls it creating "headspace." Science explains it as increasing our interoceptive awareness, which is what helps us identify needs.[2]

The truth is, we may not always know what we need until we make time to create a list. This is a written form of release, which we will continue to practice throughout this chapter. But there are countless forms of release. One of my favorite passages captures this powerfully: "A musician must make music, an artist must paint, a poet must write."[3] In my own interpretation, I say, "I do what I do because I can't *not* do it."

You may be reading this and immediately realize you need some headspace to journal. Others might recognize they need to call up a friend and open up or hit the gym for an intense workout. The advantage of building the habit of release is that it's about recognizing your unique needs and implementing practices to meet them. It doesn't have to look like anyone else's journey.

Needs vary from person to person. The important thing is to keep refining the practices that allow us to be honest about our needs and to free those needs from the captivity of our minds.

Studies show that if we don't address our needs, they can have negative health implications, including stress and burnout. The American Psychological Association found that nearly 60 percent of workers are negatively affected by work-related stressors such as burnout, emotional exhaustion, lack of motivation, and a desire to quit.[4] They cite that the first step to recovery is recognizing these issues exist. When we apply our Feeling Framework next, we will have a prompt to do this.

But first, let's consider some of the reasons we resist the habit of releasing. See if you identify with any of these:

- ***Cultural Conditioning:*** You have grown up believing that opening up about your needs is not an option. It may not be a law, but in your world, it might as well be.
- ***Perfectionism:*** Holding everything together isn't just something you do; it's who you are—or at least who you believe you should be and must be—at all costs.
- ***Control:*** Even if deep down you know that having control is an illusion, holding on is still easier than letting go and letting others in.

When we practice the habit of release, we surrender our sense of control. Releasing challenges those of us with a perfectionist mindset by recognizing, "I don't have it all together all the time; I could use some support." When we say, "I need," we relieve unrealistic pressure and remind ourselves to invite others into our journey. It takes practice to open up and identify the illusions of perfectionism and control.

We also need the habit of release to identify what we need to "let go of" or "set free"—because holding on to things that no longer serve us creates barriers to hope. Consider giving yourself permission to practice the habit of releasing today, like using your own personal gift card for time and space this week—maybe even right now. And don't be like me . . . actually use it.

THE FEELING FRAMEWORK

The Feeling Framework prompt paired with our third habit, release, invites us into this kind of liberation by completing the following prompt: "I needed . . ."

As I practice it right now, I would say,

I needed . . . to face my fears and believe in myself.

Your turn. Is there something you needed to release?

I needed . . .

____

____

The habit of release creates space for shared hope. If we don't express our needs, we can't give anyone a chance to be there for us, even if they want to. The balance is off when we carry all the emotional burdens—like worry and stress, for example—and refuse to share them. If you're unsure of what you need to release, it may help to see another example of someone who practiced navigating their feelings and found freedom in releasing.

ANITA'S STORY

Anita approached me in the hallway after one of my keynote speaking events, her trembling hands and quivering voice hinting at the depth of emotions approaching the surface. Through tears building up around the corners of her eyes, she looked at me and began sharing a profound experience she'd had.

She described how my presentation had been both challenging and transformational for her. She'd had to leave the presentation abruptly in the middle of it, due to a panic attack, explaining her social anxiety made it too difficult to be around so many people at once. Discouraged, she wasn't sure she would be able to go back into the room again.

This wasn't the first time Anita had a panic attack. They had been happening for years and were becoming a deterrent to building connections with others. As she continued to share, I looked more intently into her eyes and suddenly recognized her. "Wait a minute, I remember you," I said, surprised. "You were one of the volunteers who came up onstage and shared today!"

As she smiled and nodded in agreement, I realized this woman had a panic attack in the middle of my presentation but courageously came back and then volunteered to stand onstage in front of thousands to openly share her struggles. The Five Habits of Hope exercise helped Anita to exchange her fears for faith, leading to a powerful form of release.

Before we parted ways, we shared more laughter and tears of gratitude for the space we were able to have together. While the framework I had provided stewarded her process, it was her own willingness to step into the space openly, breaking a previous habit of withholding, that had such a strong effect. Once she acknowledged her social anxiety and the emotional pressure it caused, she took a risk, opened her heart, and decided she had something to say. She recognized the value of her own voice and was able to release by using it.

Anita felt a tremendous amount of pressure to carry her anxiety on her own. She expressed it as being a burden she had endured alone. After releasing some of the suppressed emotions she had spent years battling, Anita found a new sense of freedom, knowing she didn't have to hold everything in. Once she discovered a process to navigate how to share her struggle with anxiety, a world of possibilities opened up and allowed her to embrace hope. This was something she could intentionally repeat. She didn't have to return to her former emotional behavior patterns, where she held everything inside. She now had a new habit of releasing in her toolbox for when she needed it.

Habit #3, release, allows us to express ourselves freely, often in unconventional ways that resonate with our uniqueness. There isn't a uniform approach. It will look different for each person. The goal is to develop your own ways to let go of pressure before the balance shifts and you no longer feel you have the option to. A way to do this is by pinpointing your emotional pressure points.

EMOTIONAL PRESSURE POINTS

Pressure, as defined by the American Psychological Association, consists of excessive or stressful demands on an individual to think, feel, or act in particular ways.[5] Pressure points are areas on our bodies that may produce significant pain or other effects if they are handled in a specific way. They can be highly sensitive but, when manipulated in a specific manner, can relieve pain.

The same can be said for our feelings: We have emotional pressure points that have the potential to cause both pain and relief. However, relief requires a release of pressure. The key lies in understanding where the source of the pressure is coming from and knowing when to release it before the buildup causes harm.

Here are three questions to consider in determining whether you are experiencing emotional pressure overload and need some release:

1. Is the emotional pressure preparing you or preventing you from reaching your goals?
2. Does the emotional pressure feel crushing, or does it inspire creative solutions?
3. Will the emotional pressure bring you closer to the person you want to be, or is it steering you further away?

When our bodies carry around suppressed stories inside us (emotional pressure points) for years and decades at a time, it can feel like we are trudging uphill with weights hanging around our heels. As we move from reflection (Habit #1) to risking opening up (Habit #2), we can then find our way to release (Habit #3), where these weights fall off. Only then are we free to fully let go of what's been holding us back and embrace hope.

When we identify our emotional pressure points, we become more equipped to take the next step and determine whether they are helping or hurting us. One of the ways we can do this is through a simple exercise where we consider examples of pressure in different areas of our lives—personal, relational, and professional. When you take a look at the following lists, notice the different pressures you feel. It's great to jot down a plus symbol if you're feeling positive pressure in that area or a minus symbol if it's the opposite. Reflect on whether this pressure is lifting you up or weighing you down. Is it encouraging or crushing?

PERSONAL

- Work full-time, take care of the household, and act as primary caregiver.
- Improve time management.
- Pay rent or purchase a home for my family.
- Eradicate debt.
- Maintain an image of perfection and never show struggle.
- Improve health and fitness.

PROFESSIONAL

- Meet deadlines and create a healthy workplace culture.
- Get promoted or start my own business.
- Earn good grades or graduate with honors.
- Study abroad or learn something new.
- Earn a living wage with benefits.
- Take a year off to explore or career change.

RELATIONAL

- Take care of others all the time.
- Set boundaries to care for myself.
- Fulfilling relationships or desire to be married.
- Meaningful friendships and community.
- Ability to enjoy being by myself.

When we identify the varied sources of our emotional pressure, we may discover we have several areas that are adding pressure to our lives. This means we have compounding pressures, which I define as two or more sources of pressure building up over time. You'll see an example of this in the story below, where the writer describes financial concerns and how it impacts their family:

It was tough because I worry about how to pay for college without putting myself and family in debt. I was feeling worried and stressed.

Overwhelmingly, I see people experience compounding pressures with the expectations to perform, provide, and meet unrealistic standards of perfection. In another story shared by a student, they describe a similar despair: feeling too much pressure and not enough hope.

It was tough because I didn't want to disappoint or seem weak. I felt a lot of pressure and a little hope . . .

As they continued on, they also shared this:

. . . but I wouldn't tell anyone.

This type of resistance to release is a common response to

emotional pressure. When we refuse to release pressures that are causing us pain, they can wear like a second skin. We can become accustomed to holding in pressure to perform, to protect, to provide. Eventually, this internal habitual sequence frequents our thought waves so often that it convinces us that pain is a permanent part of our story. We can even find comfort in this pain if it's all we've ever known.

The pressure so many people are struggling with can be devastating and difficult to measure. Yet understanding the dynamics of our emotional pressure points is crucial in managing the various types we experience. Taking the time to recognize and evaluate these pressures can provide us with the knowledge needed to address them effectively, leading to a healthier and more balanced life. As we do, we may stumble across creative forms of expression along the way.

Release can come in a lot of ways. Mine came through poetry. Anita's came through speaking in front of a crowd. For some, it happens when sharing their story, something I again discovered behind bars.

HOPE, BEHIND BARS

Nearly everyone in the audience was wearing orange with the exception of a handful of press, politicians, and community organizers. When I looked out from the stage, this color was a stark reminder of the different lives in front of me. Lives separated by barbed-wire fences and orange fabric. Lives confined to the cement walls surrounding us. Some confined for months, years, or even decades to come.

This was the first TEDx event ever held in a women's correctional facility. The event was titled "Hope, Behind Bars,"[6] and it was an inside look into the hard work of restoration. It was a peek behind bars, focused on women who were navigating back toward a life of hope.

I was honored by the invitation to coach some of the women in crafting their stories and delivering their speeches. They had spent weeks preparing beforehand and had worked tirelessly on their stories of suffering, strength, and enduring hope. During the weeks leading up to the presentation, I saw beyond the sea of strikingly vivid orange uniforms. As the women shared and presented photographs of their children and grandbabies, I caught glimpses of a profound longing contained within them. These women longed for hope.

In preparing their stories, they seemed to be digging out and removing a deep-seated suffering from within. In doing so they were exercising Habit #1, reflection. After reflecting, they went a step further and took a risk (Habit #2) in opening up to the coaches and their fellow inmates who were going through the process with them. Once they started writing their speeches, they practiced the art of release (Habit #3). It was through this action of letting go that forgiveness was freeing them. They were finding peace in their pain, and they expressed it with tears of joy and gratitude, showing how external situations don't have to change for there to be hope. Even behind bars, hope's transformative power is possible.

A SHARED RELEASE

On the day of the TEDx event at the correctional facility, I was set to perform a spoken-word poem that I had been invited to write for the women there. I had first turned to performing spoken-word poetry because I wasn't able to talk about hardships any other way. It gave me, on my own terms, a sense of control in a world where I felt like I had none. This habit of releasing taught me to carve out space where I could express my emotions. And it didn't have to be in a conventional format. I could be as creative as I wanted.

When I agreed to perform a spoken-word poem for the women inmates, I aimed to embody the fire that had been fortified in my heart, to ignite an enduring hope that could spread. As I began, I channeled an emotion of reflection and then began to release it in the opening line of my poem:

> She grew up believing
> the deceiving
> voices
> inside of her head

As I went on, I locked eyes with a woman whose story I did not know. I reflected on my own shame—the kind I once would have hidden—and chose to let out those feelings through the next lines:

> The judgment, shame or pain inflicted fear
> made it sometimes easier to hear
> "you are nothing"
> "you are no one"
> and "no one could ever love you"
> than to see the disapproval staring back
> at your own reflection in the mirror

Halfway through the poem, I was struck by a deep sense of anguish for anyone suffering with self-captivity. I continued:

> For she was a prisoner
> inside of her own skin
> and it didn't matter how much hope wrestled within
> she could never quite
> find the light
> to erase all
> that buried her in

Through my words and delivery, I wanted each of the women to know how much I believed in the power of hope for anyone, no matter their story:

Nothing can slow down or hold back
a woman who knows where she is going

a woman going
above, beyond and even behind bars
to speak truth and shine light
in even the darkest places and spaces
that have tried to overshadow the sun and
    swallow the stars

For the woman
who rises
above the weight
the worry
and the world that has given up around her
is a fire wrestling with a kind of fury
that can bury
the shame that has silenced
the courage that has been held captive for far
    too long

In the end, I wanted to make it clear that hope was the common thread bringing us all together that day:

This is the kind of moment
that breathes hope into despair

and doesn't care
where you've come from or what you've done

because every breath we inhale
can propel
a new ending to any kind of story

the weight on our shoulders,
it's time to be released.

We all fall
but this is about standing back up
TOGETHER
and silencing any story that tells us this is the end.

As we connected with each other after the event, the barriers that had once been strikingly evident seemed to fade, replaced with a restored sense of healing and possibility. This was made possible because of the space created where we could exercise a form of release through the art of communication.

The habit of releasing may be the most challenging of the five habits to practice, but it is also the most freeing. It is only when we release, when we let go, that we can begin to make room for Habit #4, receiving (and, ultimately, finding) hope. As you weigh the hurdles and risks of releasing, I challenge you to consider this: What if letting go is the only way to hold on to hope?

THE ART OF RELEASE: FINDING YOUR OUTLET

Finding methods to alleviate our emotional pressure points and foster hope is essential in tackling these intense feelings, and it can be a physical, spiritual, or creative process. Sports used to be a primary way for me to release pressure. After multiple injuries, however, I began to find release through talk therapy, faith practices, and creative expressions such as writing and performance poetry.

Art transforms us both physiologically and behaviorally, giving us the emotional release we didn't realize we needed. It stimulates the release of neurochemicals, hormones, and endorphins.[7] We don't need to create art because we are necessarily great at it; we create because with every brushstroke, every note, and every dance step, we change how we navigate the world—from the inside out.

Writing can be a simple way to incorporate release as a daily practice. Creative writing habits can even increase optimism and life satisfaction.[8] For me, I could release pressures regularly, clearing my soul every time I put ink on the page. Every feeling expressed in writing symbolized the beginning of something new, pulling me toward hope. A blank page was a second chance to rewrite how my story played out. By simply making space to be honest, hope showed up on every page.

A consistent habit of daily writing applied the right amount of pressure to release my own emotional pressure points, but there are countless healthy ways to do this. It could be through dance, film, painting, or music—any place or expression where you can articulate emotions that are often difficult to convey in everyday conversation.

Self-expression can alleviate the stress of loneliness. According to Jeremy Nobel of Project UnLonely, it can improve mental and physical well-being as well as provide a sense of being witnessed and seen.[9] It even helps us connect in loss, as noted by neuroscientist and psychologist Mary-Frances O'Connor. O'Connor attested that artists can capture the nature and essence of grief, writing in *The Grieving Brain*, "Poets, writers, and artists have given us moving renderings of the almost indescribable nature of loss, an amputation of a part of ourselves, or an absence that weighs on us like a heavy cloak."[10]

As in-person interactions decrease, finding alternative approaches to communication becomes increasingly critical. Creative expression can play a pivotal role in bridging this communication gap. It's a powerful tool for people to feel connected in their most joyful moments and seen in their darkest hours. Through a creative release, the potential to bring worlds together is endless. Think of your favorite anthem being sung by hundreds of thousands of people in a stadium. It's hard to feel hopeless when you feel connected.

As we consider the increasing feelings of disconnection in a world where technology is ever more present, creative expression can serve as a method to improve well-being and create space for more meaningful, in-depth relationships. We can look to art and its creative releases as a universal language that can unify and spread hope.

HEALING THROUGH SELF-CARE

Art not only releases emotional pressure points, but it also heals. Remember, releasing something we hold in that causes pain doesn't have to be one particular kind of act. Self-expression comes in many forms.

When working with social workers and psychologists at a conference in Georgia, I admitted to struggling with having a newborn at home and being back at work. I confessed my fear of failing my kids and being ashamed to tell anyone because I'm supposed to be the expert. I have to have everything figured out, right? I can't help others while at the same time needing help myself, right? Wrong. It doesn't matter what a person's résumé or role is. We all need a process of release.

As I collected the responses from The Five Habits of Hope exercise at the event with these mental health professionals, I was stunned that the majority of them shared how they were also struggling in similar ways. One psychologist wrote, "I struggle because there's way too much on my plate and I rarely ask for help."

Others shared the pressure of working in the field, the toll of carrying an emotional load for others without an outlet for release. Hearing their stories was a reminder for me too: I need to take space to feel. In fact, it is crucial if I want to continue pouring out to others. Caring for others without self-care may work for a little while, but it's unsustainable. I hear caretakers and people of all professions and roles expressing that they sometimes feel they need to fix and solve things for everyone else, yet they never acknowledge the need for any support themselves.

Where do you go to feel and heal when you are the one providing that space for everyone else? Do you pause to think about what you need in these moments? I asked my fellow mental health professionals to brainstorm solutions. In doing so, we first had to reflect (Habit #1) on how we felt, risk opening up about it (Habit #2), and then critically think about how we can implement our own practice of letting go (Habit #3).

When I opened up to the audience in Atlanta about my feelings of guilt for being away from my family, their compassion was truly heartwarming. I had to release that guilt to process my emotions, and by tapping into the Feeling Framework prompt "What do I need?" I was able to identify exactly how to release. This moment inspired us to engage in an impromptu activity together! The room, filled with hundreds of dedicated experts, collaborated to create a list of practical actions we can regularly take to help release these feelings.

RELEASE PRACTICES

Breathing exercises	Travel
Dancing	Reading
Walking in nature	Calling a loved one
Massages	Daily devotions
Alone time	Sip coffee in solitude
Worshiping	Meditations
Free thinking	Crying
Exercising	Singing out loud

Did you notice there weren't any suggestions for spending more time behind a screen? Even though I am not sharing every suggestion collected, I can assure you "screen time" wasn't written on any of them. Distinguishing this can serve as a powerful reminder of how valuable your presence is, of what matters most. Remember, it's difficult to be truly present while reconnecting with a loved one or while taking a walk in nature, when our heads are down, focused on our phones.

Don't allow the simplicity of these suggestions to trick you into thinking they don't matter either. They aren't supposed to be complicated or require a ten-year commitment to execute well. You don't even have to be good at what you choose. It's about finding a way to let out what is no longer healthy for you to hold in.

Habits aren't likely to stick if they're hard. They need to be practical enough to integrate into your lifestyle.

The ultimate goal for approaching hope-based habits is to keep making space to connect the dots between your own hurting and hope. To do so, we must fill in those gaps with a process of listening to what is hurting us and practicing letting go of it in a healthy way. In one of my journals, I jotted down a "note to self" to remember this: You can't help someone if helping them is hurting you.

Regardless of where, how, or when you implement a practice of letting go, what matters most is that you do. The important thing is to prioritize a practice that works best for you. Find a form of self-expression from the list provided or something entirely different that speaks to you. Remember, we are developing a process to heal and have hope. Enjoy the process with a little creative expression when you can. What if letting go is the only way to hold on to hope?

YOU ARE NEVER ALONE

I needed love and compassion.

I needed someone to take notice and ask.

I needed reassurance. I needed love. I needed to be wanted.

I was needing someone to understand me.

I needed time space, support.

I needed someone to reach out and say it will be ok.

I needed something to show me that I wasn't worthless.

I needed to be reminded of who I was created by and what I was created for.

I WAS NEEDING SOMEONE TO TELL ME IT'S OK AND FOR ME TO BELIEVE IT.

NINE

HABIT #4: RECEIVE

I stayed silent because . . . everyone sees me as independent and strong.

Nothing about him made sense to me. He was raised on a remote farm, far from the nearest grocery store. I moved to New York as soon as I turned eighteen to immerse myself in the big city. He excelled in science and mathematics and learned to build a computer from scratch, while I gravitated toward people and psychology. He had a subtle and unassuming charm, whereas I was outspoken, an extroverted personality. He considered himself introverted, while I felt energized at social gatherings.

Just days after realizing I was in love with him, life brought unexpected news, and it led us to part ways. With a heavy heart, I reassured him that I didn't like commitments anyway. I encouraged him to find someone whose stability was better suited to his composed nature and traditional background, someone better than the chaos I often found myself in. I was trying to shield him from the storm within me.

I moved forward with my life, while wishing him well in his. I never thought I'd see him again. Fast-forward five years. I stood at the front of an aisle. White-and-gray lace outlined my silhouette;

I had one arm wrapped around my father's and the other linked to my mother's. When I looked up, there he was, eagerly waiting for me at the altar.

With each step I took toward him, I moved further away from my instinct to run from relationships. Our union marked a merging of our opposing worlds. It was an unlikely harmony strengthened by a force I had previously spent a lifetime resisting. Standing hand in hand in front of our loved ones, I surrendered my fears to a shared faith in "forever together." I chose to trust.

That was the day I allowed myself to take on the most challenging habit of all for me: to receive love.

The habit of receiving intersects every aspect of our lives, especially our relationships. It requires self-worth, trust, and a willingness to accept a shared hope. By practicing it, we are preparing ourselves for what we truly desire. Hope can transform our lives only if we let it in.

CARPE DIEM

After watching the remarkably complex and painfully emotional movie *Dead Poets Society*, I used to scribble the words *Carpe diem* throughout the pages of my notebooks. Translated from Latin to English, it means "Seize the day." The root origin of the word *receive* shares a similar spirit. It comes from the Latin *recipere*, meaning "to take back" or "to seize."[1]

The habit of receiving presents a unique challenge compared to the other habits of hope. Unlike emotional practices such as reflection, risk, and release, the habit of receiving is so intertwined with self-worth that it ultimately concerns self-acceptance. Before we can embrace other people—or even our own wins—we need to grow in self-acceptance.

It doesn't mean we have to accept everything offered to us. It's about preparing ourselves to receive what is *best* for us. To explore this, consider any current thought patterns you have regarding receiving. Do you question others' authenticity when they offer you something? Are you afraid of seeming greedy or ungrateful? If you were to trace as far back as possible to identify the roots of your relationship with receiving, where would they lead you?

Reasons we may resist receiving include:

- ***We don't think we deserve it:*** Compliments feel awkward, gifts seem unnecessary, and support can be overwhelming when you don't believe you are worthy of receiving them in the first place.
- ***We have* The Giving Tree *mindset:*** When you're always giving, even until you have nothing left, selflessness teeters into self-sacrifice.
- ***We don't recognize its value:*** Whether it's advice, support, or a hug—if it doesn't fit our definition of *helpful*, we won't have it.

We might discover we are great at receiving compliments but can improve on letting others support us. The heart of receiving isn't about taking; it's about accepting everything from joy and love to recognition and relationships. Receiving is an invitation to seize hope!

THE FEELING FRAMEWORK

Have you ever received a gift on your birthday that you did not want? Likely, the person who gave it to you was guessing what you would like. You probably never explicitly told them what you wanted. Unless you are like my son, who creates an Amazon wish list every year, they were left to figure it out on their own.

The way we tend to our emotions is similar. Even if we practice the other habits of hope daily, staying silent about our struggles and needs means no one knows what's happening beneath the surface. Over time, this kind of silence grows quieter. Before we know it, we aren't just silent about what we're up against; we're silent about our hopes too.

If I were to answer the Feeling Framework prompt for the practice of receiving, I'd say:

I stayed silent because . . . I was afraid to need anyone.

Have you ever felt this way? Choosing to say nothing rather than invite someone in to your feelings? Give it a try right now. Complete the following prompt:

I stayed silent because . . .

____

____

When we identify why we stay silent about the struggles we endure, we begin uprooting the spoils that quietly poison relationships. We create space to receive hope and foster genuine relationships.

I almost missed out on experiencing this for myself.

TRUST ISSUES

The greatest barrier to the hope-based habit of receiving is a lack of trust. See if you can spot a common theme here.

I didn't say anything because I didn't *trust* anybody enough to hold my grief.

I stayed silent because I couldn't *trust*.

Confronting mistrust is humbling. We need to get dirty, digging into unhealthy thought patterns and removing the rotting roots. Trust is hard for most of us. If you are not ready to process areas of mistrust in your life, know that there's no rush and you can go at your own pace and process. The goal is to recognize whether or not you are having issues with trust and then to choose whether you're ready for a process that will help you navigate your issues and cultivate hope.

TRUST LANGUAGES

Trust is an invisible foundation in a relationship. You might not see it, but just like hope, you know whether you have it. So how do we figure out where and in whom to place our trust? The truth is, we don't always know. For good reason, we can't always trust. We don't just throw caution to the wind if we've been taken advantage of, abandoned, betrayed, or neglected. There's no guarantee you won't get hurt if you trust someone.

Let's consider the concept of "trust languages," my spin on author Gary Chapman's book *The Five Love Languages*, which outlines five primary ways people express and experience love.[2] These love languages have become so popular that some people even share them in their dating profiles. This got me thinking about the need for trust languages too.

Think of trust languages as love languages tailored for those of us navigating mistrust—in any kind of relationship. While both love languages and trust languages focus on emotional needs and connections, trust languages lean on building a stable foundation from which to express love and set up our relationships for success. Trust languages foster a sense of security in a relationship so that it can express, receive, and grow in love.

Emotional Space

Recommended for: you if you've been hurt, abused, or mistreated.

Signs to look for in yourself: You might minimize your feelings, acting as if they don't matter, or become short in your responses, having little patience to talk things out with others.

It may sound like: "Nothing's wrong. Don't worry about me. I'm fine" or "Just leave me alone!"

How to navigate: Give yourself safe emotional space—a judgment-free zone—where you can process your feelings on your own terms without outside pressure.

Helpful language for your support systems: "I'll be here when you're ready" or "What would make you feel comfortable right now? Would you like me to give you some space?"

Recognition

Recommended for: you if you've felt taken for granted or made to believe you don't matter.

Signs to look for in yourself: exhaustion, resentment, bitterness.

It may sound like: "I just can't do it anymore" or "I've got this, like I *always* do."

How to navigate: This is not the time to hold back or play small. Focus on building thought patterns that elevate your self-worth and relationships you feel respected in. And make time to celebrate your resilience. Put on a party hat and buy a cake if you want to.

Helpful language for your support systems: "I saw how you did the dishes today, and I appreciate you" or "You know I love how hard you work for our family." "I'm proud of how you handle everything and stay who you are."

Presence

Recommended for: you, if you've felt overlooked or misunderstood.

Signs to look for in yourself: withdrawal, getting frustrated quickly when you aren't receiving attention.

It may sound like: "Just forget about it. I'm going to do my own thing" or "I'm done talking about this; you just don't get it."

Ways to navigate: Give yourself some of the attention you are craving from others. Be present and attentive to your own needs. Rediscover a talent you once loved to pursue. Invest in new experiences. Take yourself out on a date.

Helpful language for your support systems: "I noticed you were really interested in that song the other day; can you tell me why?" "Can you help me understand more because I want to know what you're going through and how to be there for you?" "I hear you, and I'm here for you."

Commitment

Recommended for: you, if you've felt abandoned, rejected, or neglected.

Signs to look for in yourself: being guarded, needing constant reassurance.

It may sound like: "No, I'm good, I don't need anyone" or "Are we okay? Was it something I did?"

Ways to navigate: Focus on building trust within yourself. Make small commitments to yourself and do the best you can to follow through with them. Try communicating with yourself more intentionally by writing a list of daily growth, gratitudes, and any grace you need to give to yourself.

Helpful language for your support systems: "Can we do this together?" "I'm not going anywhere; you can't push me away; how can we move forward?" "I appreciate when you communicate what you need."

Community

Recommended for: you, if you've felt heartbroken or taken advantage of.

Signs to look for in yourself: isolation, discouragement, doubting that people care.

It may sound like: "They don't really care about me" or "I don't know if I'll ever love again."

Ways to navigate: Resist the temptation to isolate. Ask yourself: *If someone I cared about were struggling, wouldn't I want to show up for them?* When you're ready, identify one person you can share a part of your struggles with. Don't go at this alone. Tap into support from people who care.

Helpful language for your support systems: "Let's figure this out together with people who love you." "You're not alone in this; we're here for you."

As you can see, lack of trust is a major barrier to receiving on our journey to hope. It can stunt relationships, prevent communication, and keep us silent. If we're not careful, we can fall into a habit of silence, a cycle that's hard to break.

THE CYCLE OF SILENCE

The late, renowned author, poet, scholar, and civil rights activist Maya Angelou remained silent for almost five years following a traumatic childhood event. Five years! Later, she wrote in her critically acclaimed, bestselling book *I Know Why the Caged Bird Sings,* "There is no greater agony than bearing an untold story inside of you."[3]

I've seen the cycle of silence in so many lives. The young high school senior who feels immense pressure to get into college while also caring for their siblings after school. They don't want to look weak, so they keep their struggles hidden. A recent college graduate who compares themself to the perfect personas they see online and questions their purpose. To avoid judgment, they choose silence. Parents who are overwhelmed with debt while trying to meet endless obligations; fearing they might burden their family, they remain quiet. Meanwhile, a newly promoted executive battles addiction but hesitates to seek help, opting for silence instead.

The insights I've gathered from the Feeling Framework prompt "I stayed silent because . . ." have been the most revealing of them all. For over a decade, I have analyzed these responses, searching for patterns and themes, trying to understand what prevents individuals who feel deep pain, like hopelessness, from speaking out about it.

I pinpointed the primary reasons for silence and refer to it as the "Cycle of Silence." This is a pattern of withholding emotions for prolonged periods, causing those feelings to be increasingly suppressed.

Consider this story below and how this individual describes why they stayed silent about their struggles.

Help. I felt alone and sad because I felt like I was trapped in my own thoughts like an endless cycle.

When we believe we can't open up for any reason, we are, in fact, trapped. And the longer these beliefs occupy our headspace, the more we extend the Cycle of Silence—from days to months to years and even decades at a time—greatly impacting our health and well-being.

In another story, we see the correlation between feeling "unheard," feeling "unhopeful," and suicidal ideation. We also hear that the reason they stayed silent is for fear of being seen as weak.

> I was struggling because I wanted
> to kill myself . . .
> I felt miserable, *unheard, unhopeful.*
> I stayed silent because I *didn't want to be*
> *seen as weak* in the heart and mind.
> I am true because I will never truly
> wish bad things upon my peers.

It can be extremely traumatizing to learn about the depth of pain being experienced by people we know. We may even feel hurt if they didn't want to disclose their pain to us. By creating spaces for people to talk and not keep these emotions suppressed or silent, we can begin to break this cycle and replace it with habits of hope.

BREAKING DOWN THE CYCLES OF SILENCE

We can't break cycles if we don't even know we're in them, and we can't remove the power they hold over us if we don't acknowledge them. Through my research with The Five Habits of Hope, I've identified five common causes of perpetuating a Cycle of Silence that can keep us from receiving care:

- Shame
- Stigmas and Stereotypes
- Systems
- Social Norms
- Self-Doubt

Shame

You know it if you've ever felt it: the secrets that linger, the regret you can't risk retelling, the guilt that keeps you from ever feeling good enough, and the lies you believe about deserving the pain.

It can sound like: "I hate myself." "I don't deserve them." "I am the problem." "It's all my fault."

Shame silenced me for the better part of my life. The shame from my past made me feel dirty for what I had been through. I imagined anyone who looked close enough would be able to see it too. I was terrified of being exposed, so I kept quiet.

Shame survives on secrecy: It gets louder in the dark. The more we keep it from being exposed, the less the voices of reason and forgiveness can be heard. The opposite is also true. Shame can't survive for long after it is exposed to the light. As soon as that thing we are hiding is seen or the past mistake is found out, there's no going back. There's no more hiding.

When shame is brought to the surface, we make space for hope to take its place.

I struggled with suicide ideation due
to being gay and Christian.
I felt alone and wanted to die.
I needed my mother's love and to
know God loved me as I am.
I didn't say anything because I was ashamed.
I am hopeful for complete wholeness and a better life
experience for other men who struggle with sexuality.

Stigmas and Stereotypes

Often fueled by fear of the unknown, stigmas and stereotypes create barriers between us. They replace potential compassion with carelessness and relationships with divisive rhetoric, resulting in false narratives and fractured communities.

It can sound like: "You're just seeking attention." "Mental health isn't real." "You don't belong here." "You're crazy." "Stop making excuses." "You're overreacting."

For years, stigmas and stereotypes led me to feel inferior, as if I could never measure up. These false beliefs caused me to hesitate pursuing what I truly wanted and made me question whether I should seek help for my mental health when I needed it. I constantly questioned whether I deserved the opportunities I worked for or if I would ever truly belong, no matter how hard I worked.

Experiencing stigma triggers a physiological response and is linked to brain patterns associated with other conditions.[4] But I've also seen the transformative power of actively listening to our unique stories. With curiosity and humility, I've witnessed how we can dismantle division and build more compassionate relationships and stronger communities. It's through these connections that hope is woven into our cultural fabric.

I struggled because of the fact
that I always felt less-than.
I felt tired of second-guessing
how I was perceived.
I needed to find people who were supportive.
I didn't say anything because it felt redundant.
I am enough because I'm human.

Systems

Always on the outside looking in. It's the invisible wall, the glass ceiling, the line in the sand—subtle indicators of a system of inequity at play. These systems, organizations, cultural environments, and institutions lack equitable resources for their communities.

It can sound like: "I'm afraid I will get in trouble or lose my bonus." "I don't want to get beat." "They won't believe me." "Just keep your head down and do what you're told."

I never wanted to acknowledge that there were opportunities I wasn't afforded because of an organizational system or the culture of an industry. I figured it wasn't as bad as my parents had it, so why should I complain? I considered it a victim mentality and didn't want to acknowledge the other factors at play in the outcome of some of my pursuits.

Over the years, I've met countless leaders working tirelessly to ensure others have equitable opportunities and access to the care and resources they need to thrive. Getting to collaborate and connect with them has shown me a new kind of system in the works—one that builds bridges for all individuals and communities to succeed.

I struggled because I was sexually assaulted multiple times.
I was feeling shame, like it was my fault.
I was needing validation and healing.
I stayed silent because I was used to not being heard and believed.
I am enough because I am.

Social Norms

Social norms represent the unspoken rules and status quo that shape much of society's behavior. Social norms are the illegible fine print of our cultural contracts—the hidden conditions dictating how we are expected to act and behave and whether we should silently suppress our emotions or not.

It can sound like: "I have to take care of others." "I need to be there for them." "I can't be a burden." "I need to be strong." "I can't be weak."

No one ever sat me down and said, "Don't cry" or "Don't show your feelings." It was the unspoken moments—watching people push back tears and respond with "I'm fine, don't worry about me."

Social norms don't need to be formally taught; they're embedded into our cultural fabric. Each norm is woven into our schools, online communities, teams, families, work environments, and places of worship. They are passed on from generation to generation, shaping how we act. But I've also seen a shift. There's a new generation holding up a magnifying glass to the fine print. They are passionate leaders who crave authenticity. They're showing us that breaking the unspoken rules of society may be just what we need to reignite hope.

I was struggling because my family that
I thought was perfect tore apart.
I was feeling angry at my parents.
I was needing to understand.
I stayed silent because I wanted to be strong for everyone.
I believe that it will get better over time and I
can use my experience to empower me.

Self-Doubt

When self-doubt hits, it can feel like there's no way out. It is what causes us to hold back, hesitate, and have limited perspectives on what we're capable of.

It can sound like: "I am not good enough." "No one cares." "They'd be better off without me."

Self-doubt has a distinct way of suffocating and shrinking my sense of worth all at once. It leads me to believe that doubt is definitive—a final judgment on my potential. But I've learned the best way to combat it is to constantly create. Each act of expression—writing, designing a program, talk therapy—is an act of defiance against doubt.

The more rebellious we become, the less control self-doubt has over us. It shrinks when we create, leaving more room for hope to take over.

I STRUGGLED BECAUSE I HAD ZERO SELF-CONFIDENCE.
I FELT BEATEN DOWN AND DEJECTED.
I WAS NEEDING VALIDATION.
I STAYED SILENT BECAUSE I DIDN'T WANT TO BURDEN ANYONE ELSE OR TRUST ANYONE.
I AM ENOUGH BECAUSE MY FAITH CARRIES ME THROUGH AND ALLOWS ME TO HELP OTHERS.

As you can see, the Cycle of Silence is fueled by everything from stigmas we hear to a deep sense of shame or self-doubt. Silence suppressed for too long can keep us hopeless. Yet sharing our struggle might be the very thing we need to break the cycle.

THE TUG-OF-WORTH: SHARING THE STRUGGLE

If silence can have such a big impact on hope, speaking up can too. In order to break free from the cycle of struggling in silence, we need to develop a new emotional pattern to break through so we can share the struggle and receive support. In the paragraphs below, I'm going to walk you through an exercise we do in my workshops.

Imagine a game of tug-of-war. Picture your hands firmly grasping one end of the rope. Feel your fingers tightening into fists as you pull the rope toward your hips. With feet firmly planted, you look up to see three of the toughest people you know holding the other side. Each opponent embodies a different barrier standing between you and your goals—overwhelming pressure, lack of confidence, or scarce resources. There's tension in the rope. Your muscles tighten, trying hard to hold their ground.

Now imagine that positioned between you and your opponents is an envelope containing a goal you've written down, along with a personal message and a surprise from me. To claim it, you must overcome these adversaries and take out the barriers. It's your strength against theirs. I call it "the tug-of-worth."

Before the tugging commences, I will ask you to rate your confidence on a scale from one to ten, where ten signifies utmost confidence. (Usually, when I facilitate this in my live speaking events, most people respond with the number two.) How confident do you feel?

Just before the tugging starts, as you get ready to pull with everything you've got, I interrupt:

"Wait. Who could help you defeat your opponents and achieve your dream?"

This is a final moment before your tug-of-worth where you get to list out loud the names of supportive friends, family, or coworkers. The first three names you say will become the force of support standing with you as you tug and pull, trying to defeat the barriers across from you. Now it's no longer just you fighting alone. It's three opponents versus you and your team of people who believe in you. The odds shift in your favor.

Now we'll let the battle begin. I count down, "three," then "two," and on "one," the tug-of-worth begins! Each team fights to stay on their feet, leaning back and falling forward, trying to defeat the other. In a final twist, I add a symbol of hope and jump in to be one more support system behind you. With your combined support, you are able to take out the barriers.

Now, before you claim your prize, I ask you to describe your confidence level again. Most people say a ten or above. What do you think caused the change in response? Almost all participants credit it to the support they received.

The takeaway from the tug-of-worth is twofold:

1. You communicate your needs, breaking the cycle of silence.
2. You share the struggle, releasing your hands so that you can receive support and trusting they have your back.

This exercise vividly captures the internal and external power struggles surrounding receiving. The reality is, you might be able to stay silent your whole life and never receive the support you need.

The question is, do you want to? When we receive support, not only is victory more achievable—the journey is a lot more fun.

Next time the odds are stacked against you, will you share the struggle and receive support?

WHAT BINDS OR BREAKS US

Up to this point in the book, we have explored hope with incredible courage. I think it calls for a quick summary. We kicked things off by reflecting on what truly matters (Habit #1). Then we considered taking a risk by opening up (Habit #2). We even went as far as releasing things we hold on to that may be hurting us (Habit #3). Next we dove into the practice of receiving (Habit #4) everything from love to support and care.

We looked at the top reasons we stay in a Cycle of Silence: shame, stigmas and stereotypes, systems, social norms, and self-doubt. Then we explored how sharing the struggle in our tug-of-worth can not only elevate our confidence when facing adversity, but be a lot more enjoyable with others by our side.

When considering any of the emotional patterns we are discussing, remember our brain pathways can be reshaped the more we practice them. We don't have to arrive at any specific outcome; instead, we approach habits as an art form. Building hope, then, isn't a lesson—it's a lifestyle choice.

YOU ARE NEVER ALONE

I was struggling with moving on.
I was feeling guilty.
I needed reassurance. I needed love.
I needed to be wanted.
I didn't say anything because I tried to cover it up.
I am hopeful because I know I'm a good
person. Someone will love me one day.

I struggled because I just got out of an
abusive relationship and didn't know how
or where to navigate the trauma.
I felt helpless and weak.
I needed support.
I stayed silent because while my
ex didn't hit me often, the mental
abuse was hard to navigate.
I am hopeful to continue my
healing and help others.

TEN

HABIT #5: REPURPOSE

I am hopeful to continue my healing and help others.

At first glance, the TRU CRU—a group of speakers I cofounded and launched my career with—was an unlikely group of individuals coming together for a shared mission: empowering youth to be true to themselves. We blended the arts with motivational speaking to connect young people in a real, raw, and relatable way.

Collectively, we were second-chancers—recovering from addictions, poverty, homelessness, and more. Several of us expected to grow up and become statistics, and not the promising kind. But we came together to change the narrative of our own lives and share the hope that others can change their own narratives too. They became another family to me.

When we initially came together, none of us had ever heard of or seen a speaking group before. Sure, we'd grown up with famous boy bands and sports teams we loved, but a speaking group?

The concept of the TRU CRU came to me a few weeks before I graduated with my undergraduate degree. I had spent the year before clinging to a seed of hope so small that most days I couldn't feel it in my grip. I had nearly been kicked out of school for my blackout, and I had spent months in a recovery program. By the time spring came around, I knew I couldn't let all the shame and trauma I had endured have the last word. I wanted to live differently. And I knew I couldn't do it alone.

I called a close friend from college to see if they would help kids in schools overcome challenges and empower them to follow their dreams. The moment my friend agreed, someone else I thought could help came to mind. Ten phone calls later, the TRU CRU was created.

The essence of our speaking group was to inspire kids to recognize they had value and worth. We wanted them to know that their voices, ideas, and stories mattered. We didn't know the science of it, but we knew that hearing our raw, unfiltered stories of humanity would spark hope for them.

The fifth and final hope-based habit, repurposing, completely changed the trajectory of my life. It gave me a chance to make better choices. It gave me hope that my pain could serve a purpose.

REFURBISHING FURNITURE

Being one of six children, I knew having brand-new furniture at home wasn't something to expect. My parents worked full-time and invested every dollar into our care and extracurriculars. But being strapped for money didn't keep my mother from having her own sanctuary in the house. We called it her "pretties room." This room, off-limits to everyone else, was filled with furniture pieces and accessories she carefully selected during her six o'clock Saturday morning estate sale trips.

To a guest, everything looked brand-new. It was as if the throw pillows and accent chairs she had spent hours reclaiming had never lived anywhere else. My mother has always seen potential in even the most unwanted and discarded items. She knows exactly how to refurbish them, giving them new purpose and a special place in her home.

Repurposing emotions is similar to my mom repurposing furniture—it requires vision and care. It's about taking something that someone else might throw away—a painful memory, a fractured self-esteem—and transforming it into something valuable to you.

Of course, there are many reasons we would resist repurposing. Do any of these resonate with you?

- ***We don't see value in it:*** Any renovation project requires vision. Without it, we are likely to go in to overtime, exceed our emotional "budget," and give up before it's complete.
- ***We fear being judged:*** Being different is often associated with being wrong or bad. As much as we want to be true to ourselves, we fear it will come at the expense of standing out.
- ***We need more time:*** We won't always be ready to transform our struggles into a story of hope. Our pain may never have a purpose. Accepting that is purposeful enough.

The most telling part of the origin of the word *repurpose* comes from the prefix *re-* (meaning "again") and *purpose.*[1] We fail a project. We fumble the ball. We forget our anniversary. Each of these moments leads to an opportunity where we can say "again." This "again" offers us a second, third, or hundredth chance to keep refining, reshaping, and repurposing.

Like all habits of hope, there are health benefits too. Did you know our brains can actually "refurbish" emotional patterns? When they do, it can reduce stress and help us create positive emotional habits.[2] Repurposing wastes nothing. It keeps hope alive.

THE FEELING FRAMEWORK

As I consider the final Feeling Framework prompt to help us put the habit of repurposing into practice, I can't help but feel grateful:

I am hopeful for . . . the next generation of passionate leaders to bring a new sense of hope to the world!

What about you? How would you answer that prompt right now?

I am hopeful for . . .

____

____

This last habit, rooted in hope, has a special place in my heart because it's the one that truly transformed my life in the most incredible ways. Repurposing is what plants a seed of possibility in places most people overlook. It transforms emotions we suppress—like shame and anger—and develops them into something meaningful. These "again" moments are where emotions are rebuilt, redefined, and reclaimed. It's another way we reshape pathways in our brains and build more avenues toward hope.

To do this, we have to set aside any feeling filters blurring our vision.

FEELING FILTERS

Those of us on the TRU CRU knew being ourselves was not as simple as it sounds. We grew up being forced to adopt a tough persona and compartmentalize who we were to fit an image and gain acceptance or, in some cases, to survive. We learned early, alongside our ABCs, how to filter our feelings. Applying filters to our feelings is a quick fix—an easy way to create distance between our pain and our purpose.

Feeling Filters remove unwanted parts and conceal what we don't want others to see. In this digital age, filters are synonymous with photo editing for social media—contouring features, smoothing out fine lines, and removing blemishes. When we filter out our feelings, we cover, alter, and even disguise our true emotions. This emotional pattern becomes a way of hiding what we genuinely feel, blocking authentic expression. With artificial intelligence everywhere—reshaping education and industries, and altering human interaction—it's becoming even more difficult to tell who and what is real.

We may hold back tears to avoid seeming weak or use humor to distract from a perceived shortcoming at work. Sometimes we might even pretend to be busier than we are to evade social interactions or to enhance our perceived value. These Feeling Filters may be protective at first but can prevent us from developing meaning and purpose in our lives. They might garner more likes and follows in the short term, but in the long haul, they can damage our health.

Suppressing emotions can drive a wedge between what we feel and how we allow others to see us. Our principles and values become scattered and compartmentalized, like a thousand-piece puzzle tossed onto the floor. This disconnection fosters a negative self-view.[3] In time, this blurs the pathway to hope and purpose in our lives. Let's investigate top Feeling Filters. Are there any you can relate to?

- ***Filter of Perfection:*** Removing what we perceive as our impurities or imperfections. Beware: Images may be misleading and appear happier than they really suggest.
- ***Filter of Strength:*** Refusing unwanted or undesirable parts of ourselves that make us appear weak. Beware of hyper-independence where seeking support is not allowed.

- ***Filter of Facades:*** Covering up what's really going on. Warning: Fun facades may likely create FOMO (fear of missing out).
- ***Filter of Fake:*** Its intention is to mislead, not just hide or distort your view. And it requires a lot of effort. Don't underestimate how quickly it becomes a double life.
- ***Filter of the Wallflower:*** The desire to remain unseen or unheard—to blend into the background so much you become a chameleon who forgets their own colors. Warning: You may lose a sense of self in the process.

When we stop filtering and start processing our feelings, the habit of repurposing can begin. Feeling Filters are obstructions, restricting authenticity. They present an image, often a distorted reality, that can hinder genuine connections and self-awareness. Feeling Filters can also be used to hide unwanted parts of ourselves or prevent something we don't want to be seen from passing through. Through them, we keep out what we don't like or aren't ready to face. What begins as protection becomes an overcorrection, in which we filter our feelings more than we process them.

When compartmentalizing our human experience—*I'll share this, but I'll keep that to myself*—Feeling Filters never portray the full picture. This becomes problematic when we desire depth in relationships and a feeling of connection. If we practice repurposing feelings instead of filtering them, they expand our lives instead of restricting them.

Repurposing requires us to be unfiltered so that our emotions can be transformed and build hope.

PAIGE'S STORY

For years, I hid my first book, which is more like a diary than a literary work. I would stash copies under my bed, only pulling them out when a client purchased or requested them for one of my speaking events. Each time I handed over a signed copy, my fingers trembled and I wanted to scream, *Are you sure you want to read this?!*

And then I met Paige.

Paige is amazing at repurposing her story and transforming it into a source of hope for others. She became a cherished friend and eventually joined our TRU CRU. Paige joined us at eighteen years old after dropping out of high school to care for her two children. Throughout her life, Paige has faced several traumas and difficulties, including domestic violence, addiction, and an eating disorder. Paige was a young, single mother living in another country away from her family. By all accounts, her situation was hopeless.

Her former principal gave her a copy of my book, and after reading it, Paige reached out to meet the TRU CRU and me. The chemistry was instant. Paige quickly became a core member, continually inspiring us. Despite facing many obstacles, including going back to school and working full-time to provide for her children, she remained committed to helping others. In time, she was ready to share her own story.

The TRU CRU had received an invitation to visit an all-girls school in a small desert town outside of Phoenix, Arizona, and Paige volunteered to share a silent skit around her battle with bulimia. The short skit included a scene where Paige attempted to suck in her stomach in front of a mirror while looking at her reflection in disgust. As Paige turned away from the mirror, she motioned toward a trash can on the floor. As she picked it up, she pretended to vomit into it. The performance portrayed the emotional and physical challenges of Paige's personal struggle with an eating disorder.

In the final seconds of the skit, Paige grabbed the trash can again, stared deeply at it, and instead of making a motion to purge in it again, she furiously threw it onto the floor. The eruption from over two thousand teenage girls in the audience was a sound I will never forget. They stood in unity, giving the most passionate applause I'd ever heard.

In less than three minutes, Paige's skit—her creative expression—communicated her story in a way that words couldn't. Afterward, we did a Q&A that turned into a celebration of Paige. Students were expressing their gratitude for the courage she displayed and how it made them feel less alone in their own struggles.

Even though Paige communicated her story through creative expression instead of a traditional format, her message of hope was loud and clear. So much so that by the time we returned home, I received a call through the hotline we had at the time. It was from a young girl thanking us for being so vulnerable and attesting that

Paige's story had given her the courage to tell her parents that she was in an abusive relationship and needed help.

Paige's silent skit spoke volumes. The impact of her bold story-telling deeply connected an entire community, inspiring others to speak up and seek support. This solidified for me the profound effect that sharing one's experiences and hope can have on others. Paige's release (Habit #3) encouraged another young person to receive (Habit #4) help, all because Paige had taken the pain from her experiences and repurposed it (Habit #5).

Building emotional habits of hope isn't just about coping—it's about taking the raw, messy parts of life and reworking them into something that not only sings but resonates with others on a profound level. The only way Paige and our TRU CRU were able to truly connect and inspire others was by doing the very thing we have discussed throughout this book: to stop allowing fear, doubt, and control to hold us back. Instead, it's about building processes to navigate the barriers in between hopelessness and hope.

As much as I felt ashamed of my first publication, it brought Paige into my life—and she never let me forget it. To this day, she shares her gratitude for that book, telling me how she saw herself in its painful parts but, more importantly, how it gave her hope for her future. She helped me realize that sharing my story had a purpose, even if I didn't want to see or believe it. That's the power of repurposing: It transcends an individual experience. Repurposing takes what's personal and transforms it into something universal—a shared bridge for connection and hope.

THE PILLARS OF REPURPOSING

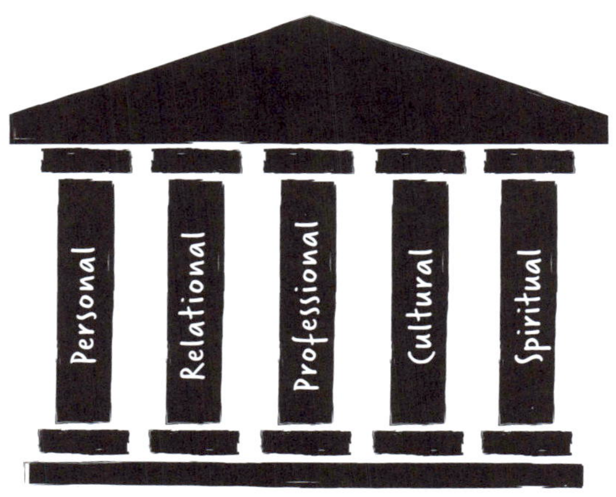

When approaching repurposing, we have five pillars to examine: personal, relational, professional, cultural, and spiritual. Each pillar helps us identify how we can apply this hope-based habit at different levels.

Personal

This pillar centers on our unique narratives. It involves our feelings, experiences, and hopes. It's about reflecting on the past while passionately shaping our future in the present. One of my business partners journals every day, saying it's how he gets through his week. As someone who juggles a lot of roles and responsibilities, journaling helps him process his feelings and channel them into a therapeutic form of expression.

Relational

This pillar involves our relationships with others. It focuses on building meaningful interactions and connections that cultivate hope. After a challenging pregnancy and delivery, a friend of mine went through the baby blues—a period marked by sadness and anxiety. She described feeling alone and scared. Once she overcame it, she decided to support other new parents by organizing meal chains through their friends and family for those early months. She transformed her own experience of loneliness into a source of joy and support for others.

Professional

This pillar overflows into our careers and work environments. It centers on uniting our professional experiences, backgrounds, and skills—sometimes for pay, other times for the greater good of the community.

In June 2020, I was working on a branding project when the death of George Floyd shook the world. The branding agency I was working with is Black-owned and led by a father, husband, and close friend. Amid the emotions and disarray of that time, he made a courageous choice: to pause all operations of his agency to support the movement and help however he could.

Instead of business as usual, his team channeled over twelve years of experience into action. Within five days, they developed a digital platform—a safe space where Black voices could share their perspectives and experiences while offering others the chance to listen and learn firsthand. With the support of friends and a dedicated team, they launched a product that reached thousands and became a testament to how combining diverse professional skills with repurposing can create something truly meaningful.

Cultural

This pillar extends beyond immediate relationships to the broader groups and communities around us. It's an approach that considers the belief systems and values that are woven into society, and it channels passion to help shape, influence, and build hope.

When I was younger, four members of my immediate family were hit head-on by a drunk driver. While everyone survived, the accident had a lasting impact on our family. My mother, determined to turn her pain into purpose, channeled her experience into advocacy. She joined Mothers Against Drunk Driving (MADD) and dedicated herself to promoting awareness and prevention efforts in our community. She was fostering a cultural shift toward a safer community through the habit of repurposing.

Spiritual

This pillar, if you practice a spiritual faith, is about transforming inner beliefs into action. It's about allowing your faith not only to guide but to actively shape the life you build.

When building a faith-based crisis hotline, I had the opportunity to work with people in my community who, despite their own challenges with mental health, were devoted to helping others. It was remarkable to see how stories of loss, addiction, and illness were transformed into powerful narratives of redemption. Hundreds of people from dozens of countries connected with our dedicated team of volunteers. By courageously choosing to repurpose their pain, they became pillars of hope for others around the world.

Building the habit of repurposing can involve sharing a part of your story to inspire someone else. It can also be a product people use, communities people connect in, mediums to share ideas through, a podcast people listen to, heartfelt emotions conveyed in a poem, and lifesaving spaces like a crisis line.

Repurposing is the way hope is activated. Unlike releasing, which focuses on letting go of emotions that no longer serve us, repurposing goes a step further and assigns meaning to our actions. When we build this habit into our lives, we are actively integrating past and present emotions into our future.

Whether personal, relational, professional, cultural, or spiritual, repurposing channels change. It takes feelings and puts them into action through projects, advocacy, initiatives, and more. These catalytic impacts build momentum for hope to spread.

HOPE IS SPREADING

Growing up in a dry, oven-heated desert, I never cared much for plants and trees. I would bask in their beauty on a road trip, but it never occurred to me that there was anything to learn from them. That is, until I married a man who came from generations of farmers.

During a recent summer stay at our family's farm, I watched as my father-in-law attached the arm of a tractor to a rotting tree. The tree had become at risk for spreading its infection to other plants nearby. After several hours and an extra set of helping hands, the roots of the soaring fifteen-footer were finally taken out. I was struck by how long and strenuous the process was to remove roots from the soil they once called home.

The more I considered the contaminated soil below the surface of what appeared to be a strong and healthy tree, the more I realized human behavior isn't much different. On the surface, we may be smiling, while deep down, we are struggling. Invisible feelings nest below the hard shell of an emotional shield. Much like the tree's roots, our feelings fight being uprooted.

When we refuse the process to heal, like the infected roots of a tree, we can spread our concealed hurt to others. We can lash out at loved ones, distance ourselves for fear of judgment, or close off the parts of our hearts we desire most to be seen. The soil is no longer safe for us or those nearby.

The struggle spreads.

This realization highlights the impact one person can have on their surroundings. Just as removing a diseased tree and planting a healthy one revitalizes the ecosystem, addressing internal conflicts leads to personal and community healing. By confronting our pain, we foster healthier relationships and build stronger communities.

Repurposing our emotional struggles—like replanting a healthier tree—creates opportunities for personal transformation. It encourages us to face our limitations and promote growth for our broader environment. Ultimately, it reminds us that nothing in our journey is wasted if it serves a larger purpose. With this understanding, we can see how much one person can influence their generation. Just as a newly planted tree contributes to the ecosystem's health, our personal transformation can positively impact those around us. We can all contribute to healthier, more supportive communities by developing our emotional processes and fostering hope.

Although the unhealthy roots of that tree on my family's farm needed to be removed, the tree still could offer value. The wood could fuel a fire, branches and leaves could turn into mulch for a garden, and the newly opened space could draw in more sunlight for new plants to grow in its place. Repurposing creates opportunities for new life to grow.

SERVING A PURPOSE

In my professional life, I'm often asked questions around people's life purpose and how to find it. The simple truth is, I never intended to be a speaker, writer, or mental health professional. It wasn't a part of any plan for me. In fact, I tried to avoid this path. I spent years speaking publicly but refusing to share the vulnerable parts of my story. I spent more hours writing than sleeping, but I didn't want anyone to know. I dropped out of school multiple times before I finally went on to complete my doctorate.

Rather than living my life trying to fulfill a predefined purpose, I focus on repurposing the challenging parts of my experiences to support others through theirs. I take the feelings that once dragged my confidence into the ground or the events that permanently stained my youth, and I create meaning from them. My aim isn't to *find* purpose but to *create* it and to build ways for others to have access to it as well.

What if our purpose is found at the crossroads of our struggles and our efforts to prevent others from a similar fate? How might you change the way you live if you believed that every part of your story—even the most painful or infuriating moments—served a purpose?

My father has always told me, "If you're having a hard time, go and serve others." This principle helped repurpose his own hardship. Growing up, rummaging through dumps in order to salvage sheet metal in 110-degree heat, he chose to make a difference and coach kids in sports after school to help keep them off the streets. He volunteered his time to serve his community in a way that he never received himself. His only goal was to serve a purpose.

In my own life, I've realized that finding a purpose isn't about seeking what's next but about serving a need. For example, I was deeply affected by the tragic suicides of two young women who fell victim to online assault. Unsure of how to proceed but driven by a need to prevent such tragedies, I immersed myself in researching solutions. This led to the development of an award-winning mobile app and an organization that hosted free community events to promote healthy relationships. My efforts weren't about pursuing a predefined purpose but about responding to a pressing need. In time, a team and impact developed, transforming a story about two young girls into an initiative that reached thousands.

The focus for me is not finding purpose; it's about actively serving one.

Repurposing pain means recognizing that each aspect of our lives contributes to a broader narrative of hope. It's about believing every part of your story has a purpose to play in building hope. And when it comes to serving a purpose, it's about your beliefs becoming louder and brighter than the dark shadows of hopelessness hovering within and around you.

THE COLORS OF HOPE

At just ten years old, she had spent several years in and out of hospitals, navigating the challenges of cancer. On the day of her celebration of life, hundreds of us gathered to celebrate the remarkable way she lived and deeply impacted us all. Both children and adults shared memories of her—how she adored rainbows and unicorns and how her hope, deeply rooted in her faith in Jesus Christ, shone brightly through everything she did.

Even amidst her diagnosis and hospital stays, she continuously found ways to express her love. Whether it was a bracelet woven from beads or a canvas vibrantly painted with bright, colorful strokes and sparkles, she could repurpose anything into magical creations, and then she would generously give them away to her family, friends, and even the hospital staff.

Her hope was a force that she didn't keep to herself; she spread it wherever she went, and it was evident at her homegoing service attended by hundreds. Despite the shadow of tragedy, the light she brought into the world doesn't fade. Her boundless and transcendent hope has forever changed countless lives, including my own. It challenged me to see that hope always has purpose, even in the midst of our pain.

YOU ARE NEVER ALONE

I dream and hope to be happy. Genuinely happy.

I am hopeful for more connection to feel comfortable.

I am hopeful because of God.

My little sister gave me purpose.

I AM HOPEFUL BECAUSE I HAVE LOVE.

I believe that it will get better over time, and I can use my experience to empower me.

I'm hopeful for my future.

I am hopeful for a better life for me and my family.

I AM HOPEFUL TO CHANGE SOMEONE ELSE'S LIFE AND GIVE THEM THE LOVE I NEEDED.

I am hopeful for my teachers.

I am hopeful for change.

I am hopeful for my personal growth and its effect on my life.

I AM HOPEFUL FOR MY FUTURE AND MAKING MYSELF PROUD.

I am hopeful for the little girls who need the help I never got.

DEAR READER

If you've journeyed with me through each of the habits of hope, you know that hope is needed now more than ever. And if you have made it this far but still don't feel hopeful, I want you to consider just one word: *maybe.*

For decades, I lived a double life—projecting perfection while feeling that my self-worth was unsalvageable. One night, I was escaping from an abusive partner and called a friend to pick me up at a nearby park. When I jumped into their car, I expected an interrogation: Why wasn't I wearing shoes? What happened?

The truth was, I had left so quickly that I hadn't even looked for the shoes. But my friend didn't ask me anything. They didn't judge, pry, or demand explanations. They simply provided me with a safe journey home. When we pulled up to my house, they turned to me, looked me in the eyes with all the hope in the world, and said, "You know, you can be anything you want to be."

That moment forever marked me. I didn't immediately believe what they said, but for the first time, I considered the possibility: maybe.

Maybe I could escape that unhealthy relationship.

Maybe I could return to school.

Maybe I could learn to have a sense of self-worth.

Maybe there was purpose in my life.

This didn't solve my problems overnight, but it created a pathway —a way to begin processing those problems. So, if you take nothing else from this book, take this: *maybe*.

Maybe might be all you need to plant the seed where hope can grow.

Dr. Julia

NOTES

Introduction

1. Edward C. Chang, "A Critical Appraisal and Extension of Hope Theory in Middle-Aged Men and Women," *Journal of Social and Clinical Psychology* 22, no. 2 (2003): 121–43, https://doi.org/10.1521/jscp.22.2.121.22876.
2. Casey Gwinn and Chan Hellman, *Hope Rising: How the Science of HOPE Can Change Your Life* (Morgan James Publishing, 2019).
3. J. Haidt and J. M. Twenge, "The Anxious Generation," in C. J. Ferguson, ed., *Childhood and Adolescence in Society: Contemporary Debates* (Routledge, 2019), 150.
4. "Suicide," National Center for Health Statistics, CDC, last updated June 2023, https://www.cdc.gov/nchs/hus/topics/suicide.htm#ref2.
5. "Depression and Other Common Mental Disorders: Global Health Estimates," World Health Organization, 2017, https://iris.who.int/bitstream/handle/10665/254610/WHO-MSD-MER-2017.2-eng.pdf?sequence=1.
6. Gwinn and Hellman, *Hope Rising.*

Chapter 2: Our Stories

1. "The 2024 NAMI Workplace Mental Health Poll," National Alliance on Mental Illness, conducted January 4–9, 2024, https://www.nami.org/support-education/publications-reports/survey-reports/the-2024-nami-workplace-mental-health-poll/.
2. Katherine Schaeffer, "Key Facts about Housing Affordability in the

U.S.," Pew Research Center, March 23, 2022, https://www.pewresearch.org/short-reads/2022/03/23/key-facts-about-housing-affordability-in-the-u-s/.

3. "2023 Overdose Report: Advocacy and Prevention Strategies," American Medical Association, https://end-overdose-epidemic.org/wp-content/uploads/2023/11/23-894446-Advocacy-2023-overdose-report_FINAL.pdf.
4. "American Adults Express Increasing Anxiousness in Annual Poll; Stress and Sleep Are Key Factors Impacting Mental Health," American Psychiatric Association, May 1, 2024, https://www.psychiatry.org/news-room/news-releases/annual-poll-adults-express-increasing-anxiousness.
5. Matthew F. Garnett and Sally C. Curtin, "Suicide Mortality Rates in the United States, 2002–2022," NCHS brief no. 509 (CDC, September 2024), https://www.cdc.gov/nchs/products/databriefs/db509.htm.
6. Thanks to the work of hope scientist and founder of Kids at Hope, Rick Miller, I now say "at hope" instead of at-risk.
7. Viktor E. Frankl, *Man's Search for Meaning* (Beacon Press, 1959), 112–15.

Chapter 3: The Social Shift

1. R. F. Baumeister and M. R. Leary, "The Need to Belong: Desire for Interpersonal Attachments as a Fundamental Human Motivation," *Psychological Bulletin* 117, no. 3 (1995): 497–529, https://doi.org/10.1037/0033-2909.117.3.497.
2. Gabriella Rosen Kellerman and Martin E. P. Seligman, *Tomorrowmind: Thriving at Work with Resilience, Creativity, and Connection—Now and in an Uncertain Future* (Simon & Schuster, 2023).

3. Ellyn Maese, “Almost a Quarter of the World Feels Lonely,” Gallup, October 24, 2023, https://news.gallup.com/opinion/gallup/512618/almost-quarter-world-feels-lonely.aspx.
4. Adrianna Rodriguez, “Americans Are Lonely and It’s Killing Them. How the US Can Combat This New Epidemic,” Health, *USA Today*, December 24, 2023, https://www.usatoday.com/story/news/health/2023/12/24/loneliness-epidemic-u-s-surgeon-general-solution/71971896007/.
5. “New APA Poll: One in Three Americans Feels Lonely Every Week,” American Psychiatric Association, January 30, 2024, https://www.psychiatry.org/news-room/news-releases/new-apa-poll-one-in-three-americans-feels-lonely-e.
6. “Our Epidemic of Loneliness and Isolation: The U.S. Surgeon General’s Advisory on the Healing Effects of Social Connection and Community,” U.S. Department of Health and Human Services, 2023, https://www.hhs.gov/sites/default/files/surgeon-general-social-connection-advisory.pdf, p. 4.
7. “AAP-AACAP-CHA Declaration of a National Emergency in Child and Adolescent Mental Health,” American Academy of Pediatrics, October 19, 2021, https://www.aap.org/en/advocacy/child-and-adolescent-healthy-mental-development/aap-aacap-cha-declaration-of-a-national-emergency-in-child-and-adolescent-mental-health/.
8. “Revealing Average Screen Time Statistics,” Backlinko, updated January 30, 2025, https://backlinko.com/screen-time-statistics.
9. Trevor Wheelwright, “Cell Phone Usage Stats 2025: Americans Check Their Phones 205 Times a Day,” Reviews.org, January 1, 2025, https://www.reviews.org/mobile/cell-phone-addiction.
10. Simon Kemp, “Digital 2024: Global Overview Report,”

DataReportal, January 31, 2024, https://datareportal.com/reports/digital-2024-global-overview-report.

11. Tori DeAngelis, "Teens Are Spending Nearly Five Hours Daily on Social Media: Here Are the Mental Health Outcomes," *Monitor on Psychology* 55, no. 3 (April 2024): 80, https://www.apa.org/monitor/2024/04/teen-social-use-mental-health.
12. Daniel A. Cox, "Why Americans Are Spending Less Time with Friends—and What to Do About It," Survey Center on American Life, December 20, 2022, https://www.americansurveycenter.org/commentary/why-americans-are-spending-less-time-with-friends-and-what-to-do-about-it/.
13. J. M. Twenge, et al, "Increases in Depressive Symptoms, Suicide-Related Outcomes, and Suicide Rates Among U.S. Adolescents after 2010 and Links to Increased New Media Screen Time," *Clinical Psychological Science* 6, no. 1 (2018), 3–17, https://doi.org/10.1177/2167702617723376.
14. Seydi Ahmet Satici, Emine Gocet Tekin, M. Engin Deniz, and Begum Satici, "Doomscrolling Scale: Its Association with Personality Traits, Psychological Distress, Social Media Use, and Wellbeing." Applied Research in Quality of Life 18: 833–47 (2023), https://doi.org/10.1007/s11482-022-10110-7.
15. Jonathan Haidt, *The Anxious Generation: How the Great Rewiring of Childhood Is Causing an Epidemic of Mental Illness* (Penguin Press, 2024), 150.
16. Christian Montag and Sarah Diefenbach, "Towards Homo Digitalis: Important Research Issues for Psychology and the Neurosciences at the Dawn of the Internet of Things and the Digital Society," *Sustainability* 10, no. 2 (2018): 415, https://doi.org/10.3390/su10020415.

17. "Warning Signs of Abuse: Know What to Look For," The National Domestic Violence Hotline, https://www.thehotline.org/identify-abuse/domestic-abuse-warning-signs/.

Chapter 4: Health and Hope

1. *Merriam-Webster*, s.v. "hope (n.)," accessed February 10, 2025, https://www.merriam-webster.com/dictionary/hope.
2. Everett L. Worthington Jr., "How Hope Can Keep You Happier and Healthier," *Greater Good Magazine*, June 17, 2020, https://greatergood.berkeley.edu/article/item/how_hope_can_keep_you_happier_and_healthier.
3. Matthew W. Gallagher and Shane J. Lopez, eds., *The Oxford Handbook of Hope* (Oxford University Press, 2018), 4.
4. Casey Gwinn and Chan Hellman, *Hope Rising: How the Science of Hope Can Change Your Life* (Morgan James, 2018), 25.
5. Gwinn and Hellman, 25
6. Shane J. Lopez, *Making Hope Happen: Create the Future You Want in Business and in Life* (Atria Books, 2013).
7. Bente K. Pedersen and Mark A. Febbraio, "Muscles, Exercise and Obesity: Skeletal Muscle as a Secretory Organ," *Nature Reviews Endocrinology* 8 (2012): 457–65, https://doi.org/10.1038/nrendo.2012.49.
8. Collin L. Davidson et al., "Hope as a Predictor of Interpersonal Suicide Risk," *Suicide and Life-Threatening Behavior* 39, no. 5 (2011): 499–507, https://doi.org/10.1521/suli.2009.39.5.499.
9. James Clear, *Atomic Habits: An Easy and Proven Way to Build Good Habits & Break Bad Ones* (Avery, 2018).
10. Richard O'Connor, *Rewire: Change Your Brain to Break Bad Habits, Overcome Addictions, Conquer Self-Destructive Behavior* (Penguin, 2014).

11. Rolf Ekman et al., "A Flourishing Brain in the 21st Century: A Scoping Review of the Impact of Developing Good Habits for Mind, Brain, Well-being, and Learning," *Mind, Brain, and Education* 16, no. 1 (November 23, 2021): 13–23, https://doi.org/10.1111/mbe.12305.
12. Phillippa Lally and Benjamin Gardner, "Promoting Habit Formation," *Health Psychology Review* 7, no. S1 (2013): S137–S158, https://doi.org/10.1080/17437199.2011.603640.
13. S. Nolen-Hoeksema, "The Role of Rumination in Depressive Disorders and Mixed Anxiety/Depressive Symptoms," *Journal of Abnormal Psychology* 109, no. 3 (2000): 504–11, https://doi.org/10.1037/0021-843X.109.3.504.
14. Aaron T. Beck, *Cognitive Therapy and the Emotional Disorders* (International Universities Press, 1976).
15. Gloria Mark, *Attention Span: A Groundbreaking Way to Restore Balance, Happiness, and Productivity* (Hanover Square Press, 2023).

Chapter 6: Habit #1: Reflect

1. *Online Etymology Dictionary*, s.v. "reflection," updated June 10, 2021, https://www.etymonline.com/word/reflection.
2. "Stress and Decision-Making During the Pandemic," American Psychological Association, October 26, 2021, https://www.apa.org/news/press/releases/stress/2021/october-decision-making.
3. Lisa Feldman Barrett, *How Emotions Are Made: The Secret Life of the Brain* (Mariner Books, 2017).

Chapter 7: Habit #2: Risk

1. Peter L. Bernstein, *Against the Gods: The Remarkable Story of Risk* (Wiley, 2012), 8, emphasis added.

2. Bessel van der Kolk, *The Body Keeps the Score: Brain, Mind, and Body in the Healing of Trauma* (Viking, 2014), 235.
3. Matthew D. Lieberman et al., "Putting Feelings into Words," *Psychological Science* 18, no. 5 (2007): 421–28, https://doi.org/10.1111/j.1467-9280.2007.01916.x.

Chapter 8: Habit #3: Release

1. *Online Etymology Dictionary*, s.v. "release," updated January 21, 2024, https://www.etymonline.com/word/release#etymonline_v_10369.
2. Kirsten Weir, "What Is Interoception, and How Does It Affect Mental Health? Five Questions for April Smith," *Monitor on Psychology* 54, no. 3 (April 2023): 33, https://www.apa.org/monitor/2023/04/sensations-eating-disorders-suicidal-behavior.
3. A. H. Maslow, "A Theory of Human Motivation," *Psychological Review* 50, no. 4 (1943): 370–96, https://doi.org/10.1037/h0054346.
4. "2023 Work in America Survey," American Psychological Association (2023), https://www.apa.org/pubs/reports/work-in-america/2023-workplace-health-well-being.
5. Pressure, adapted from the American Psychological Association's concept of stressors, American Psychological Association. APA Dictionary of Psychology, s.v. "Stress," https://dictionary.apa.org/stress.
6. Julia Garcia, "SILENCE Any Story That Tells You This Is the End," from Perryville Correctional, TEDx Talks, video July 16, 2018, YouTube, https://www.youtube.com/watch?v=dNJczYOw90U.
7. Susan Magsamen and Ivy Ross, *Your Brain on Art: How the Arts Transform Us* (Random House, 2023), 18.
8. Magsamen and Ross, 170.

9. Jeremy Nobel, *Project UnLonely: Healing Our Crisis of Disconnection* (Penguin, 2023).
10. Mary-Frances O'Connor, *The Grieving Brain: The Surprising Science of How We Learn from Love and Loss* (HarperOne, 2022).

Chapter 9: Habit #4: Receive

1. *Online Etymology Dictionary*, s.v. "receive," updated May 19, 2021, https://www.etymonline.com/word/receive#etymonline_v_7374.
2. Gary Chapman, *The Five Love Languages: How to Express Heartfelt Commitment to Your Mate* (Northfield Publishing, 1992).
3. Maya Angelou, *I Know Why the Caged Bird Sings* (Random House, 1969; repr. 2009), 189.
4. Susan Magsamen and Ivy Ross, *Your Brain on Art: How the Arts Transform Us* (Random House, 2023), 92.

Chapter 10: Habit #5: Repurpose

1. *Online Etymology Dictionary*, s.v. "repurpose," updated January 15, 2021, https://www.etymonline.com/word/repurpose#etymonline_v_40536.
2. Norman Doidge, *The Brain That Changes Itself: Stories of Personal Triumph from the Frontiers of Brain Science* (Viking, 2007).
3. Carl Rogers, *Client-Centered Therapy: Its Current Practice, Implications, and Theory* (Houghton Mifflin, 1951).

ABOUT THE AUTHOR

Dr. Julia Garcia is a psychologist, behavioral researcher, and renowned speaker dedicated to helping people move from feeling powerless to empowered through the science of mental health habits. For nearly two decades, she has worked with educators, students, business leaders, and individuals facing life's toughest moments—helping them break through fear, doubt, and hopelessness to build lasting habits of healing and hope.

Dr. Garcia weaves real, lived experiences with behavioral science to create practical, transformative strategies for lasting change. Whether on the TEDx stage, leading interactive workshops, or inside *The 5 Habits of Hope*, her mission remains the same: to prove that hope isn't just something you feel—it's something you practice, one habit at a time.